CATALYST

MY FIVE DAYS IN HEAVEN

MEGAN C. BROWN

Printed in the United States of America
First Printed November 2022
Cover Art by Victoria L. Hawkins

Published by:

Southern Willow Publishing, LLC
1114 Highway 96,
Suite C-1, #340
Kathleen, Georgia 31047

ISBN: 978-1-956544-26-8

To my brothers Raffi and Shant, you both taught me how to be a mother at a young age. I am so proud of each of you and the men you have become. Our brother Morgan is now in the place I describe in this book. I love each of you as the gifts you are to me.

To my son Lee David. I am so honored to say I am your mother. You are the reason I have felt a love in my south that is like no other. May you continue to grow and evolve as a man with patience, gratitude, compassion, love, and the freedom to be yourself with every soul print you leave with others throughout your life.

Preface

Planted is a seed in the soil that represents life. The seed will then undergo a change in fertility due to the fusion. Time makes the seed sprout in order to grow into a plant. Then the plant requires more specific needs in terms of soil, sun, and temperature conditions. Everything must coalesce perfectly in order for the seed to become a tree.

Like the tree, my soul's specific needs must be met in order for growth to transpire. The specific need for Love is my soil, sun, and climate conditions. All are conducive to the layers of Love provided by my internal source and my external sources.

Our world is filled with seeds planted in soil. May we teach the globe to love their seed so that the trickle effect of soul expansions from the outside sources flourishes throughout every home, school, religion, and everyday life. Without me and you loving one another, how will Love continue to grow as the tree of life?

It is with great care and concern for the world that I write the following pages about my newfound understanding of the meaning of life. Before I take the reader into my five-day adventure in Heaven, I want to introduce my understanding of love and the soul. It involves science, math, music, and God.

I have explained in great detail on the following pages how God and science are one and the same, and how a marriage of the two is necessary in order to understand ourselves. I am without a doubt a firm believer in God, Jesus, Prophet Muhammad, and Archangel Michael. Each has ignited my soul fire with a compassion for humanity I would never have had without my near-death experience from kidney failure in 2007. It is my hope for our world that whosoever's eyes read these pages feel love cascading down like a waterfall from Heaven into their minds and comforting their soul.

I have shared my experience in Heaven, and everyone I met with while I was there, with great ease. The history of our world has taken on a different meaning, for me, based upon the meetings I had with Gaius Julius Caesar, President Abraham Lincoln, Goddess, and Freddie Mercury, to name some. It is my hope one will take away the multiple lessons of love given to me and utilize these pages as a source for love's recipes of your own. The spiritual awakening, I have had is admittedly one sided, but with great detail I offer to you avenues into another's personal awakening with the ingredients given to me. God introduced the amazing opportunities humanity has at healing our gashed world with the understanding of our personal accountability to energy dispersed throughout the globe. It is our minds, the power of our minds, and how we choose to use them that can make all the difference.

By the power of Heaven, those whose souls have yearned for a greater understanding of life in general, it has been given on the following pages. I realize this statement is rather bold, but it is what it is.

May your lives be fulfilled with love.

Megan Brown

Chapter 1
God and the Brain

The fluidity with rigidity in science and life is required. The arch overall encompassing is a fraction, a two-piece equation, in the end equaling one answer. The fraction being physical divided by psychological, equaling individual outcome. At the time of our death, physical is taken out of the equation. The new fraction is psychological divided by individual outcome squared, which equals psychological multiplied by one, plus individual outcome multiplied by two, equals (overall psychological capacity) plus (individuals' overall response with self and others based upon everyone's life is one's determining ratio). The final answer is always multiplied by two; an undivided twinning ratio, a duplicate of energy received by self with absolute consciousness from an unchanging common denominator, thus, equaling an unbreakable triple compound love frequency.

Embodying as the galactic equalizer, acting as the arch umbrella of protection to all-encompassing every energy, force sequentially placed within the arch number code existing throughout the spherical embodiment of all that is, or was.

The French definition for the word matter is 'importance.' The English definition for the word matter is 'substance.' In popular culture, it is thought the left hemisphere of the brain specializes in such subjects as math and language, while the right hemisphere is said to retain focus with subjects of the artistic and creative realm. There is no evidence of genetic patterns confirming these differences in chemistry. A slanted view into how the brain works has suggested it as more of an informal network base, opposed to being rigid in its life purpose. Brain activity is dictated by its past experiences and current situations.

Simultaneous to our individual histories, it is a simple fact that throughout life our brains prioritize development with coordination-oriented tasks yet must control billions of neurons and an equal number of cells receiving/storing this information throughout the body. Science today cannot completely explain how the human brain thinks or why. There is a sequence of code letters in DNA (Deoxyribonucleic acid) currently existing and inactive throughout the entire volume of the brain. There are multiple types of RNA (ribonucleic acid) active within the brain. As an introduction to my hypothesis, I will introduce the heterogeneous nuclear RNA any class of single-stranded nucleic acid molecules of ribose and uracil found chiefly in the cytoplasm of cells, in certain viruses important in protein synthesis, and the transmission of genetic information transcribed from DNA. (Random House 1991)

In recent years, the human atom has been thought of as a positive life force. Each has animatedly come to life in the human body in the childbirth process. Because of

A Catalyst

our parents, guardians, and/or caregivers, we envelop our surroundings through experiences by which we are introduced, thereby following the ways of every individual in charge of cultivating our life journey. We are being prepared for an inevitable role change throughout humanity. Every single individual, depending on where in the world we are raised, will categorize individual responsive reactions to individual experiences, thus portraying a difference in qualities through our interactions. What we know, and how we come to know, is truly a recipe from life experiences! Every moment in every experience creates absolute consciousness, universal consciousness, individual consciousness, and multi-level consciousness within the brain. As I was told in Heaven by Hippocrates, the brain composition is a fractionated compound of multi-layered grids. There are five grids, to be exact: the whole brain, gray matter, white matter, protein, and carbohydrates.

The whole brain is the primary receiver, coordinator, and distributor of information throughout the body. A split-brain is one in which the connections between the hemispheres have been disrupted. Named gray matter, simply because it is darker than white matter, it is the part of the brain containing myelinated nerve fibers. Gray matter is a type of neural tissue that contains nerve cell bodies. It forms most of the cortex and nuclei of the brain. The white matter is the insulation that covers those nerve fibers. Proteins are essential components of the muscle, skin, and bones. Proteins and carbohydrates each provide four calories of energy per gram. An enzyme consisting of amino acid residues joined by peptide bonds, protein is one of the three nutrients used as energy sources (calories) by the body.

Megan C Brown

Carbohydrates are one of the three nutrient compounds, along with protein, used as energy sources (calories) by the body. Complex carbohydrates come naturally from plants.

The Fractionated Compound

The English definition for fractionated is non-existent. Heaven's definition is described as follows.

A fraction, by English definition, is a part. The subtext date is defined on these pages as being in English what we know as an anagram, a type of wordplay, or a nickname. Before I build the rest of the word fractionated, I must define the word compound. In this breakdown, it is defined as being a mixture. A fractionated compound is part of a mixture below the threshold of conscious perception capable of evoking the seminal response. A seminal response is generative. Think of the generative as being a preparatory school, seminary, or a learning process, especially for higher education. A fractionated compound is like a subliminal message that concerns the brain. The compound or mixture being an application of mostly DNA accompanied throughout with the spice of my individual life, meaning my life is preparation.

Stepping into my childhood for a moment, I remember seeing for the first time a certain music video by a young man known as the "King of Pop." It started with him leaving a movie theatre with his date and ended with dancing in a graveyard with the dead. This is one of my many connections to music and science. What registered brain pattern was stimulated by his freedom in having stepped outside of a once confined way of entertaining the masses?

A Catalyst

I have never spoken to the man, and if I had, I imagine the dialogue as being basic; elementary in every sense to him by how simplicity was seamless in his exquisite display of music and dance. He evoked my mind throughout with immediate disbelief of virtuoso characteristics enlivening my previously dark thoughts of a graveyard, with an unconventional dance accompanying my excitement viewing souls emerging from the soil that buried each of them.

My individual feeling about this music video gave me hope. My mind's response to his lack of inhibitions was necessary to recognize what development transpired as a reaction. My life journey forward was assisted by a music video, created precisely to ignite a new avenue of soul expression. Whether or not it was part of "The King of Pop's "plan to give me his imprint on my soul is irrelevant. His spark ignited the start of communication with me.

Scientists have learned that they cannot completely understand the role that gene activity plays in brain function until gene expression patterns are measured in individual brain cells. The entire physical body is absolute consciousness. Throughout every living organism and thinking, humans alike animate the physical body they inhabit. How can some scientists propose generalizing the brain when the life experiences registered within everyone's mind are usually contrary to many portrayed circumstances that were created by familial and societal geographic locations? Having stated God's theory with my human comprehension, it is obvious to me the division within humanity can never be corrected without proper direction. The success rate of individual countries throughout the world relies completely on the participation of the populace, or the dictatorship ruling every individual's outcome.

What I am describing, in my opinion, is universal consciousness. A scaled-down version of the universe at best, but vitally necessary to initiate the freshness of awareness, having enormous rudimentary advancements for an entire global effect benefiting every participating individual. Having said this, I am aware of the influence that consists of religion throughout history. A rhythm of being has consistently driven nations, countries, and states into liveliness throughout humanity's successions of defeats. Individual consciousness is its life vibration. An individual thought manifests energy throughout the physical body, mind, and soul. Enigmatic dialogues throughout history have taken over rules once created for the continued purification of humankind. Deception in persons everywhere has granted trust within accumulations of mind to obtain victory within the ego's self.

By way of God's orders, I was forced to watch the outrageous behaviors annihilating tiny pieces of happiness throughout humanity. Only tiny on the global scale of humanity, every tiny piece of happiness became uncontrollable flames touching off a domino effect of emotions ignored by humankind and rippling ferociously throughout generations upon generations. Every emotion being fed differently based upon location, a time in history, and whether the individual was directly affected. Our history, whether it be personal or global, has directed us over time in a recapitulation of brain range being undiscovered due to lack of understanding what the obvious question is. Is it a lack of global compassion to have such would require every individual to hold themself accountable for every thought, action, and

A Catalyst

reaction performed? Or, is it a lack of empathy for my state of being? It should be a requirement of mine to empathize with myself, to identify with me, for I must know who I truly am. How am I to identify with a Muslim in every sense of the word without knowing the source of each of us?

Love is a fraction divided by reality. Aligning my mind with my soul is my choice, yet simultaneously the determining answer. Placing love in the mathematical equation explained to me in Heaven, it reads as follows:

My mind is two chakras, my throat is one chakra, and my torso is two chakras. The number five is the number of applications per existing grid in the universe. My universe being earth as a moving energy grid enabling every frequency applied by way of a mysterious glue. My mind, my throat, and my soul are the trinity of love. When aligned, the other four will unite automatically. The triple compounded frequencies of love are unbreakable. My feet chakras give me the ability to create the movement of my body forward, backward, diagonally, or sideways. My productive and reproductive self is a part of my nervous system. These chakras are unable to move without direction from my brain. What I can do, how I choose to be, how I choose to integrate within and throughout begins from the confines of my mind. To transport energy purposefully, I must understand completely what I have just said.

Humans have been deceived by fear compounded generationally. Previously barbaric civilizations consumed societies by engulfing the minds of the peaceful occupants; brutally executing traditions of existence to progress disdain into previously tranquil minds that once flourished throughout the world. My mind was once tranquil until the reality of my surroundings became dangerous. The only protection I knew became a withdrawal from self to relieve my mind of the pain stagnating. Unguided and unknowing of self-worth, it became paralyzing throughout my entire human body. The human body builds itself. Mathematics could help instruct us in constructing the world within as being fixed by participating in an unchanging method using soul intuition, almost seeming paradoxical and contradictory as a result of our limited understanding of love being the inner structure of the geometric figure each of us is.

A plane figure, made up of lines and volumes of planes, is an unchanging foundational composition based upon the triple compounded frequencies of love each of us embodies. An unbreakable frequency consumes our entire being, making each of us the most powerful method of mathematics eternally. My understanding of the self became the forefront of my mind when I was faced with examples of acting as love's expressionless example of being while watching my life review.

Nuclei express exact genes that are primary structures such as the hypothalamus, the hippocampus, and the pans clustering in distinct groups, which are each different from one another. The structures I just mentioned intertwine with the laws of science.

Understanding that the laws of science are derived from the archived Love Laws will ultimately change the role of gene activity in individual brain cells and the overall measurement of brain activity. Gray matter overall becomes the largest playground for frequency productions. Not just any frequency; there is a hardwired preprogramming within the gray matter. To shed light on what I refer to as being the gray matter frequency board, reproductions, including exterior ways of incorporating

A Catalyst

the soul through incarnations, must occur. There is a soul dialogue currently in pause mode due to circuitry disconnections resulting from every individual's inability to hear the musical composition of love that has been silenced globally. A brain's full capacity of activity cannot be fluent in the dialogue of love without the mind's ability to regard the silent agreement of aligning itself with every sharp note played on the galactic grand piano, that is of a most stellar celestial composition on account of two notes never played before. Love's trinity realized will keep mobilized the most powerful science eternally.

I have accompanied my way of being with religion, science, a music video, and mathematical equations. A new question I propose to myself is, "How is it these four sections in my life overlap at all?"

How am I to understand what was preached in church, what was taught in my science classes, what I visually absorbed from a music video, or achieved an answer to a mathematical equation I had yet to have been given any numbers for? How does each integrate easily and overlap without exception, while being a constant production of outcome for all? One day these questions entered my mind. I began to write about what I thought the answers were based upon the balance within my life. Then I had to ask myself, "What balance?"

Values of self became my next big question. It is impossible to understand values in humanity without direction back to the source: my soul. Then the question to myself became, "What is my soul value?" This question requires me to listen to the individual rhythm I am for the accompaniment is love. My lacking understanding of the truth creates my inability of equality within, not to comprehend the likeness of self, equates a definitive possibility of being the characteristic of terrorism within that the outcome would create discrimination against me. My room inside the confines of self can develop my physical reaction; an understanding I am faced with continually, all of this I had done unknowingly literally without awareness resulting from being without guidance.

My love for humanity will go on with harmony and fluidity within a rigidity of science that is my life-an arch exists covering the entire fraction. It consists of a two-part equation that in the end equals one answer. The fraction is physical over the psychological, equaling individual outcome. At the time of one's death, the physical is taken out of the equation. The new fraction is psychological over individual outcome cubed, or divided, equaling psychological multiplied by one plus individual outcome multiplied by two equaling (overall psychological capacity) plus (individual's overall response with self and other) (= sign with a line down through the center means equalizer as being) (based upon each individual's life is one's determining ratio) the final answer is always multiplied by two. An undivided twinning ratio, the duplicate of energy, received by self with absolute consciousness from an unchanging common denominator equaling an unbreakable triple compound love frequency that is the galactic equalizer being the arch umbrella of protection to all-encompassing that is every energy force sequentially placed within the arch number code that is throughout the spherical embodiment of all that is.

One day while visiting a friend, she was driving us to a clothing store to look in. We did not make it to the clothing store that day. Instead, another store, an antique store, caught her eye while on route to the original location. She quickly turned into the parking lot and parked the car. We were excited by some of the vintage things we could see in the window. As we walked inside, we realized this store was much more than an antique store. It was sectioned in such a way whereby we could decide what era to look at first, clothing, furniture, books, jewelry, and art. It felt more like a museum to both of us. At the end of our two-hour stroll in the store, one piece caught my eye. It was a ceramic, white human head. Written in black over the head was a calculation breakdown over sections of the head. The name on the front below the face was LN Fowler Phrenology Head. I looked closer and saw letters forming a word inside each sketch of form, each in the section location it was written. I felt as if I was looking over the synopsis chart describing developments in a brain. It showed the names, numbers, and locations of the organs.

#17 indicated spirituality, #19 benevolence, #23 mirth, #33 time, #35 language, manners, and language in behaviors.

Phrenology is a science that established a link between the morphology of the skull and the human character. It was Franz Joseph Gall (1758-1828) who discovered the brain as being a housing unit of all mental activities. Gall's main work is "The Anatomy and Physiology of the Nervous System in General, and of the

Megan C Brown

Brain in Particular." He made statements regarding principles in his book.

- Both moral and intellectual behaviors are innate.
- Exercising or manifesting is reliant upon thought.
- A brain is the primary organ of every propensity, sentiment, and skill.
- A brain's overall composition includes organs, emotion, and skill.
- The form of a head symbolizes the formation of a brain and results being associated with the development of the brain.

The laws I have listed above were considered the entire science by which phrenology was built. Gall tied together exact pieces to explain one's character and precise brain locations on each hypothesis. Gall's mentor was Johann Spurzheim (1776-1832), who had successfully spread phrenology in the UK and the USA.

During the early 19th century, a progressing interest in phrenology grew. The science of phrenology was abused byways of commercial purposes. The emergence of phrenological parlors dictated science as being similar to astrology and palmistry. The science of phrenology was disrespected even though it was constructed on the foundation of science.

It was the LN Fowler statement I read in the antique store that made me curious. It read, "For thirty years I have studied crania and living heads from all parts of the

12

A Catalyst

world and have found in every instance that there is a perfect correspondence between the conformation of the healthy skull of an individual and his known characteristics. To make my observations available I have prepared a bust of superior form and marked with the divisions of the organs following my research and varied experience." The first question I asked myself after having read this was, "How has this concept been overlooked?"

I believe that a balance within requires active participation on my part with a central knowing of fairness and truthfulness to achieve an honest positive concentration for love. For my yo-yo performing abilities to happen by way of my mind, I must direct my hand participation with my brain and a complete understanding of what goes up will fall for good without directing it back up again based on my knowledge of science, or gravity prevailing without energy exchange.

My race and gender are what I was born with; it is only a part of who I am. It does not define my life in any way, nor should it be the definition of anyone's life. "Where is the Love?" is thought-provoking for sure, but the question is not answered. How can it be answered when no explanation of love exists?

While driving home after picking my son up from school our ears perked up when the beautiful song "Where is the Love?" started. As I listened to the words and my son singing along, I began to feel the excitement within and throughout my body. Music was asking about love; the keyword being about! The word about suggests learning, then it all hit me at once. I thought of a way to explain my near-death experience that would unify every soul within humanity, without unintentionally chasing away the peace-loving individuals who make no claims to religion.

The Black-Eyed Peas and Justin Timberlake assisted me in figuring out how I could introduce and explain the scientific ingredients of love. They became my catalyst to merging science and love, my experience in Heaven, the wisdom from the father of medicine and respected philosopher Hippocrates, and God. It was a specific line, 'turn the other cheek,' that caught my interest in understanding the world as having separated as a result of religion for the feeling of comfort every soul innately reaches for.

The race is defined in English as meaning pursuit, running, or speeding. Nothing in the definition in any way indicates skin color on the human body, color is defined as a pigment and shade. Again, this English definition does not attach the definition to a human body. How have these two words dictated such extraordinary hate throughout our world? By definition alone, exclusion of others makes no sense. Every individual must be held accountable for their participation, right? It would seem so, but lacking the required skills puts all of us unfamiliar with love at a greater deficit. With no hope of positive change, a mind can automatically recycle old paint as the outcome. This is a sad reality plaguing humanity throughout our world. How can I tell my child a change will happen if the whole of humanity is without instructions? I must first teach my child to accept all ways of being as the way to learn different life philosophies. Individual philosophical growth throughout homes, communities, towns, cities, societies, states, countries, nations, and our world requires unified participation. I hope my near-death experience sheds a light on different ways of being from current realities that have yet to be

A Catalyst

introduced to science. Until God and science are married as being the same, an endless cycle of segregation, separation, and distribution of hate by personal choice is certain.

The song mentions terrorism in the world. It points out specific groups who have, to date, portrayed themselves as fearing what lies outside the home. Why should we fear what lies outside of the home when it is our minds dictating reaction to that which we do not know? Our minds have indicated what is going to happen. We have told one another, outcomes-based upon what? Only perceptions from some who in some way put an end to other questions by way of characterizing a collective whole as being a genre who in one way or another has seemingly been given some sort of superhero power that will take over and destroy a town, a country, or the world. Superhero indicates having extraordinary powers that are used to help protect others, but the supervillain must be stopped.

The villain is defined as being an evil person. Throughout world history, numerous leaders were villains who in my eyes are supervillains. Each used their power like that of a magician in my opinion. A magician merely suggests that a natural effect has been made visible to the mind; a structured and manipulated comfort of the mind. In having accomplished the suggestive way it is, and the approach survives throughout the audience, the final act is ready to be revealed. It is in the outcome of the final act whereby it would seem the mass of onlookers will approve or disapprove amidst the individual's character conditions that become pressure mounting throughout the magician's mind. It is the audience who determines whether the act will be successful. Getting back to our world history, it has always been the people who determined success. The success of every civilization was achieved because of a leader who understood the power of every person's mind needing clarity.

It is the superhero whose magic tricks are supernatural. Super as being excellent, incomparable, magnificent, marvelous, and outstanding to name some. Natural as being everyday happenings keep going because survival is a predetermined course within the confines of not only a mind but living situations as well. Then one should ask themselves if a natural-born life is an indicator for every individual's choice and outcome. Everyone's life is a derivation of time from life experiences. The word emotion becomes every individual's superhero or villain. If we are not taught to love ourselves during post-production of choice, support will be lacking throughout the entire foundation of self. Without the ability to support self the outcome is quicksand. The mind has every reason to fall into the sands of time as it becomes the hourglass holding all the days of our lives.

If only I knew how to write myself a new leading role. I don't want the magician part of the villain, and I do not want to be a background character in my own life. For my goal of loving myself to be reached, I must memorize my part and be the person I was born to be. If I do not know who I am, the onlookers in my life will not believe me.

A solid script of who I am is what I need. If I do not understand myself, it simply means I do not understand my message during this period in my life. How am I supposed to express a feeling still not obvious to me?

Before I can commit to a job, I have to get answers from the producer concerning an overall end story. What

A Catalyst

is expected of me must be clear to me for feelings to come up inside of me. For me to be the character I am, I must know who I am.

I must broaden my reality of production to make a point. An executive producer's job requires fundamental knowledge of the long-term expectation for the continuing project. If an executive producer commits it would be their role to make sure production stays inside of the budget that is based on a schedule.

A screenwriter chooses development with a story based upon knowing firsthand perhaps a suggestion concerning what the creator envisions the project as being. Truly the most important source for needed information. The job requires the creation of dialogue, characters' roles, and the storyline. This position requires an extremely well-versed life for attempting to inject all of humanity with a message.

For a film to get financing, the originator must begin pitching the idea while developing a concept. The investor needs to notice a value for the project before post-production can begin. A project value is therefore each unemployed crewmember dream. The value must resonate with a current subject matter or a historical subject matter that continues to weave itself into current day importance.

For a historical subject matter to hold the attention of an audience, the subject must contain a humanitarian message opening a human wound that has not come close to healing.

The talent agent must listen to the industry's needs. A role is a person who finds jobs for actors, screenwriters, musicians, directors, and producers. This role defends, supports, and promotes their client because the agent believes the ability of their client separates them from all other applicants applying for the same job. The agent is a third party between the studio and the client. It is the agent's position to negotiate for a lucrative future contract benefitting both the agent and their client. A need for an agent can categorize an actor's value if the agency representing the actor holds power within industry standards.

An accounting department for any form of production is the one whose job checks and balances profits and expenditures. Estimates in revenue for every production rely upon every individual's costs and future anticipation of the public response. There are many avenues in production accounting, but in the end, it is how much money is put out and how much money is taken in after everyone has been paid.

Why have I explained the most thoroughly possible creationism of a project and a few essential key players in giving life to an idea? This is everyday business for many forms of production throughout the world, and it seemed on the nose concerning comprehending everything that went into the Black-Eyed Peas song. As I thought about the song's title it became the center of a metaphorical puzzle, I had been given so many pieces for, but I realized a construction of this kind is without using every piece given to me. The obvious question to me is in the song title, where is the Love? The subliminal message is, in my opinion, about our world being segregated, separated, and broken. How do we as individuals help heal the entire globe if every individual does not notice the lack of love being expressed? If a person's vision is impaired, it requires a trip to the optometrist who will determine what help is needed to see again. Based upon my visuals while I was in Heaven, I felt the lack of sowing me into the fabric of world love. Without the information, how is

A Catalyst

a loving capacity to be understood? With no instructions, how can a love like the one I felt in Heaven be obtained on earth? In addition to my near-death experience, this one song made me think about being responsible to love.

Slavery is a reality that has and continues to act as a human gauge for an individual's value in the world. For anyone to make malicious decisions based upon a person's skin tone that's derived from genetic ancestry, using God is the most mind fucked justification I have ever thought about. This thought alone indicates no love, no matter how protected or comforted a mind is by religion.

When I was first greeted by Jesus, I remember His beautiful smile, His welcoming behavior to me, and the rich brown color of His skin. While Jesus had unconditionally welcomed me, He did not continue with an additional fact that because I look Caucasian, I would be treated differently than others with darker skin color. Jesus did not racially profile me. Earlier I mentioned how humanity classifies one another from a race or color. Neither definition of the words races, nor color, pertain to the color of the skin on the human body. I find it to be knowingly offensive as a human that the status quo could be different. Some birth certificates require the race of each parent and the parent's occupations. It is interesting to me how "race" and "occupation" slid in with a standard operating procedure format. This is a state-by-state decision in the United States. This fact is an arrangement of racialism being figured in the greatest form both figurative and literal. When I think about what President Abraham Lincoln, Rosa Parks, and Dr. Martin Luther King, Jr. did to demand fairness and equality within humanity, the birth certificates requiring "race" and "occupation" would be insulting to them and should be to every human being. If I am to believe in a reason for something to be made different, everyone's common denominator must be seen and felt. All of this to say a common denominator exists in every ordinary unit of the mathematical system. Science has shown math as being the common denominator by which all the science calculates every finding for every scientist.

Without a global understanding of the A, B, C's, and 1,2,3's, there would be nothing linking humanity to medicine, automobiles, aircraft, boats, and architects. Rome was not built in a day, and neither is this breakdown I have methodically with great care and concern put down on paper. I hope to help create an understanding of the necessity of the new rhythm in what could be our unified world. Just one song created within me a cascaded free form association in my thoughts.

It might surprise many and maybe none that there is intolerance in Heaven concerning segregation. After I was welcomed by Jesus, He took me into the golden capsule where I was met by another group of beautiful souls. I did not see one Caucasian body in the room with me. There were three I will describe as being with a nice, golden tan; the kind of tan I remember lying on a towel on the beach to achieve. Below the equator, a golden tan is achievable for me only after nursing myself back from a painful sunburn. These souls I stood before were not wearing swimming suit attire. I imagine the race box on their birth certificate indicating 'other' with an explanation next to it as being Armenian, Yugoslavian, Serbian, or Israeli. There was one soul I will never forget named Archangel Michael. His dark skin color would require a check in the box stating His being African American. No way was Archangel Michael going to allow the 'n' word, or any form of discrimination, to anyone. I

A Catalyst

remember what He did to my soul without placing a single finger on me, not to mention, I recall a photo in the Catholic church of Archangel Michael keeping Satan's face down with his foot. I cannot imagine how He would correct a situation that included a genetic insult directed to His body or anyone else's.

With absolute respect to God and His kingdom, I would describe God's genetics as being from perhaps Yugoslavia. His skin hue and His voice seemed to me as being from an Eastern European region. If He had to check a box, I think it would be 'other' as well.

Beginning with genetic inspiration from a set of birth parents who for whatever reason united in a life-bearing commencement that gave automatic origin in an ancestral coming together way only, is meaningful on a driver's license, a job application, or when moving to another country on earth. Heaven's application for entrance is only reflective of an individual's manner of conducting oneself throughout one's life. My life review was indicated before me in a documentary format. In my transmittal, my guides and I watched with firmness how I participated in my role as self. Was I being myself, or trying to please another for acceptance of others, helping myself or others, and did I in any way give love to myself or others? There were many pauses throughout the viewing. A moment of feeling an emotion followed by an immediate question regarding what I was thinking and feeling in the scene displayed before me. Communication with my guides was mandatory. I cried, I threw up, I laughed, and felt a rainbow of feelings. When we were finished, I was led to the Synagogue where I had to sit amongst a diversity that included wings. If a shade of skin on a body was the determining factor for my sitting

Megan C Brown

at God's table, the darker skin hues and wings all
outnumbered me.

Chapter 2
God and Numbers

I have been brought to life by a· near-death experience in Heaven in the most unorthodox way.

Superheroes, villains, a song title, a music video, a yo-yo, phrenology, math, and science are all participants concerning my ability in explaining an experience somehow, someway, no one has ever explained before. I have used subjects I know as being common throughout our world to generalize people's lives in such a way that makes it easier to understand Heaven's message/the book/my story. Every story was brought to life within a structured format with my hopes of connecting a person with a way of being. Writing from my perspective, only I know everyone as being a creation of science. With a purpose for an explanation as a creation of science, we are all creators in a creative sense. My goal of a superhero concept is relevant in every way. Just like a superhero, I must be flexible with myself (such as how to deal with unexpected obstacles) every day. Life tends to present itself as a child on the playground who suddenly trips and falls. Through the child's reactive response is an indication of what kind of attention will be needed. Just like a fall, life has a way of happening. The ups and downs throughout every day cannot be planned. If I had the power to control the remaining course of my life, then I would be neglecting other's lives who are involved within the overall outcome of mine.

A significant factor is the threading of humanity stitched into the same fabric that is love. Completeness of self, in my opinion, is inclusive of patience, fragility, sensitivity, honesty, fortitude, determination, and the ability to surrender to each circumstance as it falls into my lap with forcefulness. The result of its arrival will determine my reaction.

I intend to speak on these pages a truth that is in the simplest way I know how to bring to life what I saw (experienced) in Heaven. My visuals depicting how I experienced Heaven and my interactions with each soul while I was visiting bring to life an incredibly powerful government that is dictating a way of being, regardless of my individual opinion. According to God and Heaven, every religious congregation, political congregation, and every educational system that ultimately produces a grown-up child affecting everyone's future must receive love's rules (laws) through whatever method necessary.

It is exciting when I think about a future that could include a global unification. To achieve unity, we must work together from the same set of instructions. Confidence in every regard has determined the outcome in every situation throughout history. Am I suggesting we are more powerful than we give ourselves credit for? Yes! In my opinion, the power of self is always bilateral, and my question becomes bilingual. Heaven's language involves every and all languages throughout the globe; a language of love that is a composition of both math and science. Heaven's language is unilingual in the outcome

A Catalyst

affecting everyone's life being one's determining ratio. The equation of fluidity within rigidity is an uncompromised way of being. If each of us adheres to the strict rules of acceptance of difference that is required of each of us, then there would be peace throughout the world. It sounds so simple. Heaven's language is love lingual and unilingual because God speaks every language. The human language has multiplied through countless years as the axis that is mathematics in every way. Love, science, and math are our skeletal axis and the second cervical vertebrae that is communication. The landlord is a communication who resides as the quiet tenant famous for unwavering in its support beneath the truths as the speaker dealing with the subject.

What is the true essence of peace? If it were the unilingual composition that is music, therein lies a magnanimous solution with results still being a virgin to that which we call mother earth. The labor pains toward a democracy for equality of rights and privileges are the multitude of examples being an unnecessary struggle throughout the so-called civilized heart of humanity experiencing constant palpitations inside of earth's main fault line that intersects congruent triangles of or about two numbers concerning one another expressing limitless mathematical formula equations, but there is only one exacting mathematical equation. That equation contains a rule and principle in times that are often of one method for any song's rhythm. The audience response is like that of the congruent triangles that hold all collections of units, being the number that is solely and exclusively having to do with an entirety that is made up of diverse elements. A multitude of borrowed ideas is the one foundation that is the common denominator in every soul that ignites the plugged-in code of ethics. Jesus Christ himself is an energy form equivalent to that of a compounded equation being exactly aligned within Himself as one unit in solid communion with love. Where there is love, therein lies peace. Prophet Muhammad is equal in all ways to Jesus Christ as a compounded equation being exactly aligned within Himself as one unit in a solid communion with love. Prophet Muhammad is one of life's examples of being a peace treaty. He was by date of birth only standing in favor of love long before Jesus was born. It should bring great comfort knowing with a timeline of ancient history, peace was at the forefront of the Middle East when Prophet Muhammad made known His thoughts and reasons as a philosopher. When this fact is realized throughout our world, only then will we know holiness that is a unification being in love's distribution. If each of us is to understand we are a number, not by birth, but given the exact denominator that will be divided by our own given number throughout our lives at the moment of death, quality and state of being during the interim could be congruent. The number three hundred represents every human. As I have already pointed out, the second vertebrae inside of every human body is the communicator. Each day is aligned with the number three hundred as everyone's unchanging denominator. It is the numerator, or version of self, daily through my life lived as a process of logical thinking, and production of creation given out consciously or unconsciously in every day that I need to focus on. Because of what I was told in Heaven, it is my opinion we are as an individual a science and mathematical formula that helps determine each other's outcome. We are individual in our thoughts but simultaneously linked to every individual energetically by the laws of the universe.

A Catalyst

In other words, we are accountable for one another's outcomes.

I want my numerator to be as low as possible. The lower my numerator means the more love I am involving in my day. A zero is perfection and holds the three billion triple compounded frequencies birth cycle of love waiting to be reincarnated in me. The inception of self-love awaits me every day from the moment I wake up to the moment I go to sleep.

The word power suggests being a force with an ability to direct and make a change. Using myself as the guinea pig, a most definitive change has occurred throughout my way of being in my life. I am more cognizant of the difficulties in my life, and I have given each one a purpose to include them on the mosaic that is a composition of another kind. For one scene in my cartoon to be brought to life, it takes multiple cells layered on top of each other to create the depth of perception for the viewer. My clarity in seeing myself will bring about a clear view for everyone I interact with to see me. I am a mere fragment of peace. One of my pieces of the structure I am is named peace and love. This is humanity. We all have the pieces. Let us all achieve clarity of these fragments each of us is and reconstruct the statue that is a state of being: Love.

To unconsciously pass through my life at this stage of the game is proceeding up the mountain again while holding a stoned head gathering only moss aligning itself while covering the entire foundation. How can I return to Heaven and defend a cop-out plea? As my luck would have it, I can't.

A star search united with my molecular force acts as my density, being a contact to that which is my soul's tied origin already grounded to a way of being, throughout the unstressed parts of an aggregate of structures situated within and near our orbit assisting, supporting, and protecting the axel leaning toward a rotation in a singular turn to correct the current course of direction of the planet earth. Each star is the exact ratio of each soul that is tied to the hitching post from the beginning amount and a total quantity of the molecular structure. A star is unified when each has aligned itself during rotation along the fault lines of the entire rotation throughout the galaxy. Unification of every soul that is, may put together a previous specific chart indicating perfect patterns of unification having been aligned as higher in rank, authority, and power. Beams that are multitudes becoming connected with the united galaxy of governments no matter what immediate squadron unites removing love, peace, serenity, and tranquility from unions of galactic compounds. Anyone possessing a desire that is considered to be counterproductive to overall superiority existence of love, peace, serenity, and tranquility will bring about viewpoints concealing essential criteria for disease to enter a purified formation of colonies throughout multiplying donors supportive of the only entrance going into the deep, immeasurable space, gulf, and cavity regions of all that is. Cavity regions are multitudes of borderless origins connected by invisible material substances equaling the ratio of watchful repetition translating throughout the dexterity circumstantial diversion of the industry into the love, peace, serenity, and tranquility efforts.

To drive illness from the body, specific flooding of music that is the compounded love frequency of 528 Solfeggio frequency carried in the formulated geometrical figure that is also the invisible material substance that translates especially watchful neutrons

A Catalyst

gathering all around, as would our rhythm into especially watchful collections within a surrounding covering the entirety, break away from soul's attachments bound to a completed grid throughout every universe, and every galaxy. Volumes combining volumes of wave patterns numerically placed inside the vault of time that exists subliminally, producing intensities that will design a course occurring inside the hieroglyphs symbiotic, interdependent relationship, of self-realization inside one's mind that will translate throughout the energy field that formulates within every cell particle.

Just as a cell in animation constitutes one frame, so too does the corresponding power within the body records data being transferred as information. Where there is no clarity, there will be an overlapped cell that is a smaller compartment and a binding of cells incongruent within the formation of the whole. This group acts as a unit within the organized compartment. Without organization, there can only be chaos. Chaos can destroy the fluidity of peace within a precious organization of a singular cell. A ripple effect executes performance and maneuvers that will take center stage throughout the entire body. Where chaos becomes the central focus, the body can only react as the audience member. Multiple titles are franchised within the self. Chaos can only continue to take over as the ringleader if one's mind allows the circus act to take place. When a mind does not understand how valuable and sacred it is, the outcome is a result of no comprehension of everything that is. If one's mind forfeits a birthright of director, producer, screenwriter, agent, executive producer, and editor of self, how will it participate? A decision is in the hands that reside with, and in the existing formatted structure already a creation, of math, science, birth parents, God

Megan C Brown

and Goddess, Holy Spirit, Galactic Master, Absolute Controller, and the perfection within the alignment of a mosaic of a symbiotic hieroglyphic composite of the musical composition that gives contrast inside of every formed triple compounded love frequency that is a soul's birthright entering the foreign territory that is life.

When a rising phoenix appeared before me, I found out it had to recreate itself without any understanding how ashes can be representatives for starting life from the ground up. I have looked at my every open wound while I was in Heaven and wondered what my numerator was while I was watching my life play in front of me. Then I quickly noticed how during my life I detached from myself. I wanted to avoid feeling pain to such a degree that I wound up unconsciously completely disconnecting from my life. A numerator cannot be achieved in disconnect mode and it does not equal zero. Why is it love that will be my savior in the end? If God is love, imagine the magnitude of love that is ruling our ruler. Whether or not I believe in God is irrelevant. In no way am I contaminating a reality I have seen and know is ruling my outcome: Heaven. Before 2007, I thought it to be more along the lines of a fairytale. Now that I have been there, I will have to check the box that reads 'believer.'

Chapter 3
Heaven's Philosophy

The nearest I have been to all extremities of self has been limitless from my near-death experience. Without guidance in how to connect with my feelings derived by circumstance, I was incapable of connecting with my soul. My soul is the historian whose purpose is to preserve my true essence. To comprehend me, I must engage in my feelings. Phrenology has brought to light another language of self.

Soul talk is becoming more and more accepted. The concept of specific energy residing within our bodies holds credence by way of science and math. Creationism is the prodigy that has scientists thinking in terms of speculation and curiosity about the origin of the solar system. Speculation and curiosity are the question mark beginning for an existing mathematical equation that is always in a state of action, by way of energy. The formula is an asserted occurrence in a specific group of phenomena that has yet to be established as fact; the phenomenon as one is a fact. It is also noted as being beyond what is usual, ordinary, regular, or established. It is superior in every way because as one, it stands out from

Megan C Brown

what has already been established. The phenomenon that has happened to me is personal cognitive development. I now recognize the participation of myself as being an exercise of opportunity including decisions made from choice. The power of choice must be recognized first to establish the responsibility of self.

For any occiput fundamental principle to correspond with animals, the human head must first understand it is considered as being the central headquarters for thought, memory, understanding, and emotional control. How will science correlate any link to animals when the human body cannot understand the completion of self? The mathematical formulation of the human anatomy has not been fully splayed as the equation it is, so recovery from early developmental months in the womb cannot be obtained. Without a complete understanding of a human's anatomy that incorporates existing order within the brain that is inclusive of an existing road map of conscious brain family indications of existing conditions, any link to animals is benign. What phrenology created by years of study are indicators of self-being connected to the internal grid that is a metric unit of measure as chambers being the origin, or main artery, to a mathematical and scientific volume already existing harmoniously as a silent agreement. Phrenology has given harmony to the mind; a realization of ingredients is fundamental to every being containing the where with all the behavior. When humanity comprehends the road map for defining conscious humanity, only then will we heal.

As with every form of exercise, conditioning includes repetition. Using healing as the mandatory exercise to be performed daily requires the brain to participate in a scaling of deposits. Emotional pain

A Catalyst

brought on through life circumstances, situational occurrences, and a calling forth of understanding to the inevitable question: why?

I was instructed by love to reexperience my life when I watched my life review. In having done so, I have come to know my participation in that regard as being an audience to my movie. Participating as an onlooker who has already experienced everything in the movie takes the slap effect out of my experience. For me to self-soothe, I must distinguish to myself that what I am required to watch is my history, and I am removed from the pain because the occurrence has already happened. I have indicated to myself I am safe. I realize in my viewing I would have handled some of the situations differently if I had known then what I came to know through self-reflection. My ability to self-reflect is by my decision only. No one can make me change; I must want to change.

There is a subliminal linkage to self and is a language currently unspoken throughout the world. The language is a simple knowing of purpose, sounds monumental really. All I must know is the basic formula of my soul that is a creation from love's perfection. A soul range of being allowed to be separate from the human body is the numerator. The numerator is a constant fluctuation like the stock market; every soul is a fraction. A rise or fall is a result of self-reflection, which requires me to connect my mind with my soul that is a projection to every memory I know as formed from the mind. My movie projector is my soul that is the archive of every incarnation from my origin of inception being my first birth. Before my first birth was a cell formation consisting of a group of triple compounded frequencies that ignited when additional data was being added in the conjugation

Megan C Brown

of the act with absolute intent of expression to another of love.

My common denominator with humanity was always the mathematical equation based upon science. How can the truth in Heaven's philosophy begin to emerge throughout the world with current existing partisan ways dictating each life in a religious, political, and public shared world? Partisan is indicative of bias agreements everywhere. From a biased perspective, a view is prejudiced, unfair, partial, influenced, and ultimately splinters from multiple minds who have never been understood, and have somehow vindicated themselves in having formed an ignorant way of being amid humanity.

Will there only be marginal outcomes as a result of disclosing a specific piece of my life. I can hope every mind that gauges my story will begin to make sense of their creation of living. Remember there can be no life donation consisting of an interest in living when life can never be lived without understanding the value in every component as being outcomes of science and mathematics throughout the history of humankind. Mathematical equations are necessary for procreation. How can anyone refute the power in love? In my life, I have experienced sensational moments of nothing more tempting than my physical response to the force of love's energy harmoniously converging throughout me.

It is my hope every other individual soul gleans a way back to soul self. The discovery is amazing in all ways. My archives consist of a fraction that applies throughout humanity, yet I am a sole contributor reliant on the entirety of our world.

Chapter 4
Heart and Soul

There is a saying and a song called "Heart and Soul." Such a calming thought about two very misunderstood forces of energy. A collaborative method to an individual's health requires animated frequencies to come together in unison as carriers for the betterment of the human body. How is an organ reliant on an unseen ball of energy? The heart is always associated with love. What predominates the other? The question should be suggested as a metaphor for the basis of humanity. It is with great concern the subject was brought to my attention by Hippocrates. Hippocrates shared many philosophies with me as we sat at a table together. I remember two very specific topics. As He approached the table I was sitting at, His presence was subtle. The time assigned to me was a wealth of information about my illness, alternative healing, essential oils, quality of mind, and the Hippocratic Oath. Hippocrates began informing me of how difficult TTP-HUS is within the human body, but due to medical advancements, my condition would be remissive. He continued to inform me of God's creation of plants, coconuts, flowers, trees, dirt, herbs,

Megan C Brown

and sun. Each was created for the procurement of civilizations throughout the world. The concept of rehabilitation for humanity has unfortunately subsided as being an unremitting form of existentialism. Philosophical visions range from one side of the spectrum to the other. There are obvious contemplations about three lengthy facts concerning the creation of fruit juice being used currently to assist the insulin levels in each human body and accompanied by the synthetic rate of occurrence. Synthetic states of assistance alternates per unit of time of a wave oscillation. In the interim of synthetic assistance, a lesser volume of the same inhibitor preventing the emission of power currently weakening the human body's natural resistance is needed for prevention of a possible breaking away from a time-released process to accelerated healing. The assistance of things from nature may seem ludicrous and absurd to think about, but what is absurd is relinquishing what dates to the dawn of time. In many ways, humanity has proceeded to hand over to someone else every power of the mind. Unconsciously, humanity has penalized itself by neglecting its birthrights to the clarity of individual thought. One's ability to employ self instantaneously in almost any great opportunity throughout existence is organic in nature. Behavior patterns within humanity are many, but less than one hundred. This figure makes all formations equivalent from the beginning of time into the current. The purpose is to register the totality of a force given guidelines inclusive of a human body's ability to plant itself anywhere in the world; a natural qualification of repairing itself with the provisions originating from the location that contains all necessary agricultural resoluteness within the confines of one's actual stock. Every forbearing organism has rapidly processed itself

A Catalyst

through yielding to an environmental locality. As horticulture is guarded by its surrounding environment, so too is the human body aided by its surroundings.

I have experienced many doctors, nurses, surgeons, anesthesiologists, and dentists. There is a handful I can speak of by name for reasons about professional integrity. Only one holds a spotlight as the exceptional medical doctor, plastic surgeon, a pioneer in the treatment of burn wounds, general surgery, was president of the Los Angeles Society for Plastic Surgeons for eight years and was an active member for multiple medical interdependent and united actions for victim category. Dr. A. Richard Grossman M.D., F.A.C.S., I am noting as being a maverick. He had an air of distinction, dignity, and eminence throughout the medical world. I knew him as my doctor for a few of my surgeries, but his demeanor overall set standards for all doctors I have seen since.

One of my surgeries, when I was thirteen years old, was under Dr. A. Richard Grossman's care for rhinoplasty. He did the surgery for just about free of charge. The car accident I endured at age nine had automobile insurance coverage that paid minimal compensation for any needed additional healthcare obtained resulting from the accident. This surgery was painful for me, as it entailed the repair of six individual breaks.

My experience with Dr. Grossman was not just surgical, it was psychological as well. The day after this surgery, Dr. Grossman came to check on me. He was wearing blue jeans, a ranch-style top, and cowboy boots. It was perfect attire for my young mind who grew up with a donkey in my make-shift backyard. The first words to come out of his mouth were, "Did you get the license plate number?" I looked at him in a clueless manner. He continued, "Did you get the license plate number to the semi-truck that hit you? I'd sue him if I were you. You look like shit."

How Dr. Grossman knew my dry sense of humor is still perplexing. I began to laugh and replied, "Please don't make me laugh. My face hurts so bad." To which he continued with another one-liner, "Whatever you do, if you get up to use the bathroom, do not look at your face in the mirror. How am I supposed to put you back together again? Let me look a little closer." He leaned forward and kissed me on my forehead. "Don't worry. I did a great job at re-breaking your nose." He began to look closely at my eyes. "What are the nurses bringing you? Do I need to talk to them? I want to make sure you heal under my watch. Tell me when anything strange happens again. My staff needs to remember you're not twenty-one yet."

Dr. Grossman had me laughing without restraint the entire time. I was so happy to have had some comedic relief, even if it was pointing out the obvious. That was in 1982, and in 2007, Dr. Grossman took my phone call. I quickly reintroduced myself and proceeded to explain why I was in the hospital again. When I told him it all started with C-diff colitis, he quickly interjected, "Oh, you must have had a shitty experience," to which I laughed.

"That's one way of putting it. It didn't end there, I got TTP-HUS," I followed us. He said, "Well there's nothing I can do. People usually die from that." I replied, "I know, and I almost did. I want to know if you have any advice for me." He thought about my question for a moment and then said, "You need rest. Listen to your body. I've never had a TTP-HUS patient. I had a patient who while in surgery showed signs of TTP and I took care of it immediately. What I've read is not a lot because it is

A Catalyst

such a rare autoimmune disease. Doctors don't know about it. I wish there was a way I could help you, but I don't know what else I can do." I thanked him for taking my call and then our conversation was over.

I made another call to Dr. Grossman in 2010. Again, I reminded him who I was. This time I boldly requested his assistance in getting me seen quickly in a certain world-famous clinic. He politely instructed me on how to get on the waiting list. At this point in my life, I had seen so many doctors who didn't know what to do with me. I politely replied, "Dr. Grossman, I want a letter from you on your letterhead with instructions of how you want a particular doctor to work with me. I don't want to wait six months to be seen. You are the red-carpet treatment. I want the red-carpet treatment, Dr. Grossman. I'm so tired of struggling to be understood."

He kindly responded, "I'll do it."

I was elated. He always helped me as his patient. He never let me down. I thanked him and shared my happiness for another few moments. Then I pointed out I had just read an article about him recommending burn victims have a family area specific to the burn center. How patients not needing an I.V. are treated in a hyperbaric chamber. I complimented him on how much of a genius I thought he was in having pioneered this way to help burn patients heal in a non-invasive setting. He quietly replied, "It's what I do, babe." My response was a quick laugh because I didn't know how to respond to such candor being spoken in a most sincere habitual manner.

Chapter 5
Medicine

When I was young, I was introduced to a few different philosophies. To some, this statement may sound so unaligned, and before my near-death experience, it seemed so enlightened. It is neither. I have broken off from everything previously anchoring me to what I knew as being my life. It has given me the understanding and courage to override all previous self-induced stipulations. An awakening of this sort has broken my mold of how I view the world. Where I once felt an ascension as being only my pushing a boulder up the everglades, my ascension has become the breaking open of my shell that I constructed as my protection because I had no other recourse. My recourse of love was lacking fluency entirely in my mind, lacking indicating being without. The world is without knowing its real power innately intertwined throughout by protons, DNA, photons, oxygen, fibrinogen, and clioquinol. My meeting with Hippocrates introduced this enzyme as being the bipartisan to mitochondria. The true power source of all energy is currently undetected by scientists due to the blood code inside cells multiplying throughout

Megan C Brown

the fibrinogen levels. Every fourth level GBH diagnosis is unfounded. GBH is known as a nervous system depressant. Its undetectable trace elements are more forceful than any modern microscope. For science to advance, the theory of relativity must include a most scrupulous performance to include calculus of the human body. The human body is ninety-seven percent oxygen and water, and the other three percent is a solid mass coalescence and cohesion of bones. Calcium is a mineral-building compound not yet equated as being a translated mutation of the triple compounded highest love frequency that courses through our anatomy automatically. A hormone-triggered compound made by the body to be released during high-leveled physically strenuous activities. An achievement of such a structured task within the human body is accelerated with physical endurance, but the key component of all acceleration is originating from the brain cortex that does not currently exist how I am describing.

Historically, medical diagnosis is determined as being a final prognosis. "A" indicates one. If only one course is viewed, maybe a handful of others, there are existing loopholes due to uneducated prudence. Individual discretion to the patient is unfortunately a major motivator. Bias and bigotry have diagnosed humanity, therefore changing outcomes of study overall. Our ancestral line is lengthy and begins in Africa. What is unquestionably true is the human need for debate. When the debate has finished, the endorphins have been worked out so completely in the mind, that the body translates the mental workout as being food for thought. The food is our inner choreography of blood particles that lines everyone. I have explained Hippocrates's history lesson to me that included the human origin explanation

A Catalyst

beginning in Africa. I did not question the Creator about why He started in Africa. I felt it best I look at Africa as an answer to the question of why vitamin D is the only crucial resource that is lacking throughout entire regions on earth. The only vitamin to be administered from the sun is vitamin D3. When Hippocrates shared with me the necessity for natural growth within an individual's medical outline to be inclusive of the local surroundings, the sun being the most vital component, to each healthy body being nourished with the essential vitamin D3. Without proper levels of vitamin D3, a human body cannot sustain the cell marriage of each molecular constitution. It is impossible to come together as the harmonious convergence of a highly functioning human body. Science has made this a fact. Science has also proven an orange to make over the possession of an illness brought on due to a diet lacking in vitamin C. Vitamin E is a deficiency of the mind's ability to procreate memory. Brain damage beginning signs include deterioration of brain cells. A body must absorb iron to avoid allergies inside societal conditions. How do societal conditions trackback to Africa? The stomach originated in Africa. When it was communicated to me that Africa is my origin, I eventually understood by way of a phrenology head in an antique store and a "Black-Eyed Peas" song the actuality of all given to me in Heaven, but I did not know what to do with all of the information. Why bother engaging with a world of onlookers spinning around like the whirling dervish?

A term from the Persian word ascetic means unflappable. Saadi was a dervish who was known for having written, "Of what avail is frock, or rosary, or clouted garment? Keep thyself but free from evil deeds, it will not need for thee to wear the cap or felt. A Darwish

Megan C Brown

is in heart and wear the cap of Tartary." In classical Persian, Evangelion is defined as effortlessness. Effortlessness is involving the exertion of physical and mental power. Great effort is necessary to achieve a feeling of victory. To obtain ease in achieving one's victory, one must continue to exert one's self as being the source of all answers to every world problem, from a source of fidelity in observance to duties. Duties include researching what we do not know or understand.

In what regard do our souls unify? I have explained every soul as being a beacon, and that each emotion in our soul is felt during each circumstance. Love does not evaporate. Love can never abandon the soul. It cannot because it is a derivation of purity. The soul is required to participate in each event. Every occurrence being significant to our creator in all forms of returning to the source. The source being loved fullness.

Just as vitamin D3 ignites the human body, so too does love to the soul. My new understanding is of love awareness needing to be executed for serenity within and throughout for universal peace to happen. It is possible to reignite a mind with peace, but it requires work and skill. Skill is acquired with persistence to any craft. Persistence requires the dedication of self to become a master of anything. When the connection of self is felt throughout the body, the metaphorical ignition of soul fire begins. Soul fire of love is immeasurable to anything; memories of happiness ignite a soul fire as well.

How one chooses to topically coat emotional pain is ultimately by one's design. I'd like to reflect on my rhinoplasty surgery with Dr. Grossman. Not only did he interject some twisted humor, he injected me with happiness. A memory of physical distress thus tied me to laughter with a tinge of pain. Pain endurance becomes a

A Catalyst

little more tolerable with a link to humor. Humor is known as the ameliorator of the body. Thankfully, I can squeeze forth under pressure a few memories. The one I love to turn to is when I was informed of how I looked like shit by my medical surgeon who had reconstructed my nose. Not only did he share with me repulsive humor, but he intertwined a glow of his soul fire with me. At my young age of thirteen, I had no understanding of a soul, but my youngish years of the late thirties into my forties has given me limitless stories of soul understanding from which came complete records of self-soothing. When I think back on my many personal tragedies, I am grateful to be able to look beneath the ashes of destruction and see a light of a different kind and the light I see must be admired. It was turned on by serendipitous awakenings. The kind of awakenings requiring one fortuitous skill for survival from historical collaborations to be threaded in such a way that creates a slanted view to probably anyone else witnessing the same situation. Perfect conditions for the brewing of another kind, where I have found the greatest comfort in many of my circumstances, is when I dial into unexpected gifts that keep on giving. Gifts that include a healer who gave me a reflection of himself. Pain with innate knowing that what I needed was a distraction with amusement of clever conditioning, softening the course of an extremely brittle physical reality. Here I was as a young child whose fortune was received from a doctor who was priceless to the spellbinding philanthropic efforts of his kind. He broke through the red tape of proper attire, bucked the system when he asked me, the underage minor, if I had been drinking, and continued to pioneer a groundbreaking procedure for the most horrific form of pain from flames ignited by a diverse origin.

Megan C Brown

I recollect a surgery on my face when I was eleven. I shared my room with another young girl who had no visible signs of scars, and I had to ask her why she was in the hospital with me. She told me she was burned over eighty percent of her body when her nightgown caught on fire from standing too close to the stove. The next morning, we were each taken for our surgeries. I remember being awakened after my surgery by our phone ringing endlessly. I opened my eyes, and when I turned to reach the phone, I saw something I can never forget. My roommate was covered in blood from her shoulders to her ankles. Covering her skin was white gauze in the color of red, covered by what looked to be saran wrap. Nothing I had experienced could hold a candle to that. I had not experienced care as a patient yet by Dr. Grossman, and I don't know if she ever had, since we were not in his hospital.

Fast-forwarding to today, I am appalled at the response of the world to the loss of such a life force inside the medical world, whose personal philosophy of another was definitely responsible for the change, and incredibly necessary for the medical field being forced to shape and reshape. Without his vision of wellness for every social and cultural civilization, we would be required to endure only skin grafting as the be-all-end-all of possibilities for each burn victim. Why I have not been greeted at the checkout counter by any magazine cover with his face on it is beyond me. His legacy and his impact is beyond every Hollywood babe splashed across any cover. It is wrong to point the finger at only one country because it is a global epidemic. While looking at the eye-catching covers is something to do while waiting for my groceries to be scanned, I have asked myself if personal lives are any of my business. Then I must wonder if they feel

A Catalyst

violated without cause. Then I redirect my focus back to the checker who has rung up my total. Then I think about Andy Rooney, whom I grew to appreciate even more so with his questions, "Did you ever wonder why?" Now I am faced with the exact question. I am wondering why such an enigma of medicine was shadowed by airline tragedies; one perplexing question has yet to be answered. Why has the complete belief system of humanity been and continues to be relinquished toward others' ways, others' lives, others' families, others' styles, and others' thoughts? Did you ever wonder why as individuals we, for the most part, try to be congruent with the latest common way to fit in? These questions direct my attention to science and math.

Human behavior seems to be indicative of animalistic survival skills. This would indicate Darwin's theory perfectly. The evolution of fish to humans could not have happened. It's, well, impossible. The ocean is a world unto itself. The ocean is so far from being understood as it is to suggest humans, dogs, gorillas, and giraffes are extensions of the ocean is ludicrous.

By way of choice, we have forfeited individuality to appease others in our surroundings for survival is not being talked about. We judge far too quickly to self-soothe, where knee-jerk reactions are common. They are determining factors of the outcome that began as a need to soothe the giant question mark that originated because of unfamiliarity, an unknown, and not knowing how to behave now. Animalistic ways of sniffing through every new feeling are brilliant, very quickly all their senses are awakened. Every trigger of past experiences is revisited immediately. In one moment, it is determined that the situation is safe or not. To give Darwin's theory the attention it deserves will assist the validity he was suggesting, to begin with. The group mentality is throughout the water world and land world. The mind pattern of safety in numbers being innate is unchangeable.

For the individual to have a sense of stepping apart from the mainstream, he or she better be ready to experience the metaphorical sniffing by the civilization surrounding. In the end, sniff by sniff, each is snuffed out for the disturbance of a group's safety in numbers theory. The aftermath will be, might be, a new route in the same direction. Solo artists tend to be very solid when each has stepped out of rhythm. They must be willing to explain a decided approach as to why any other group fed soul should, or would, consider a fresh approach to a new normal.

I have often wondered why humanity has relied upon individual plight as being directed from one symbol. What is symbolic for one might not be for another. When symbolism meets adversity to its origin, those preventing propagation will multiply by natural reproduction amidst the chaos, difference, and overall change throughout entire societal structures. The question becomes: Who will take the place as being the overall foundation of the new formation? Why is there an innate need to follow some sort of symbol to feel valuable? The symbol is just a symbol, after all is said and done. So, what is with altruism having been pushed away? To quarrel about specific symbols throughout humanity suggests internal and external manners of behavior don't jive. This is significant in that it starts from one place.

Fear disassembles innate behavior that dictates the very essence of every soul. Love is primordial; it began as the only existence making it timeless. How has

A Catalyst

timelessness been erased as being the supreme ruler? What is timelessness? I thought there was only one ruler, God. Will the new ruler include everyone?

Love is the supreme ruler. In the beginning, it was love for every creation blanketing the universes and galaxies. How does one symbolize a universe or galaxy, perplexing to say the least? What if the beginning was simple?

Chapter 6
Einstein and Our Beginning
"The Creation of All"

Love is a fraction divided by my life's reality and multiplied by love's reality.

Goddess asked Jesus to bring me to Synagogue to meet with Her where God had previously met with me. Goddess smiled at me with gentleness and asked me to be seated in the chair She pointed to. Jesus pulled my chair out for me, and I sat down in it as Goddess had instructed me to do so. Jesus sat in the chair to my left between Goddess and me. I couldn't help but look at Goddess and wonder why I was in Synagogue this time. I was not prepared for the amazing story I was graced with.

Goddess began, "There is very important information needing to be included in the book God has ordered you to write. The mystery of the thirteen crystal skulls is linked to the Mayans, and this is partially correct. There are Mayan prophecies for 2012. Earth knows about December 21st, 2012, but they do not know why. You will tell them Quetzalcoatl, who is also known as being a feathered serpent, informed the Mayan chief during a visit about the thirteen skulls and why they were created. They are 'Love's Protection.' They were left by Quetzalcoatl whose actual name is Isa. Quetzalcoatl presented Himself as a seventeen-foot tall white seraph and created what is known today as the Pyramid of the Feathered Serpent. Inside this pyramid are hieroglyphs replicating what is inside of a blue book; the same blue book Quetzalcoatl also appeared to and gave the chief of the Mayan tribe. Quetzalcoatl inscribed a love-matching layout inside of the blue book as hieroglyphs defining 'love's protection.' On the floor inside of this pyramid is a hieroglyph of the feathered serpent handing the chief the blue book. The chief never spoke of the blue book again, so as not to put the book or the holy experience in danger." Goddess paused and asked me, "Do you have any questions?"

I laughed out loud with excitement while tilting my head back, "Where is the blue book with the hieroglyphs inside of it?"

Goddess continued, "It is interesting you did not ask about the pyramid. Why is that?"

I replied respectfully, "God ordered me to write a book, and now You are ordering me to put this information in the same book He ordered me to write."

Goddess smiled and said, "I am devoted to protecting love as well. I can never say where the blue book is located."

I smiled at Goddess and politely replied, "I have been surprised in ways I didn't know were possible. Heaven has opened my eyes and taught me anything can happen. I am curious about this seventeen-foot tall seraphim."

A Catalyst

Goddess and Jesus both smiled sweetly at my response. Jesus began, "There are three seraphim in total. The white seraphim are named Isa, the lavender seraphim you would know as Father Time, and the teal blue seraphim is named Aaron."

"Wow," I said, "Love is a constant in Heaven, but are people going to believe what you are telling me?"

Goddess smiled and said, "We have our ways."

Jesus said, "I love, Megan. Is this truth taught on earth?"

"Yes," I said.

Jesus continued, "You will be introducing instructions to a concept that is the power of love for everyone. Love is the supreme ruler."

I leaned back in my chair with my hands in prayer position over my nose and mouth. The information they just explained to me was beyond amazing. It was as if a metaphorical master key had been given to me and it was turning on my soul fire. They want everyone to be ignited with this information.

I said, "Each story of love keeps getting better and better. How does one love story surpass the effects of another love story?"

Goddess continued, "Love gets better and better, Megan. Love is limitless and leads me to the next piece of this story. I would like you to picture the number ten. The number one sits before the number zero. The line creating the zero represents limitlessness. The line contains the frequencies of 'Love's Protection.' Love's Protection unites everything. There are three billion individual love frequencies inside the zero that are the seeds of love. Please close your eyes and visualize your fingers anywhere on the zero lines and break it open. Line up one end of the zero to the top of the number one, and the other end to the bottom of the number one. Now each number is parallel to one another. Each number was different but is now united. Individually these two numbers are considered limitless. Now each is united and most powerful as the limitless number one. The outcome is 'Absolute Love Protection.'"

Jesus began, "You may open your eyes now. Please, for a moment picture two zeros next to one another creating the infinity sign. The limitlessness of this symbol is compounded. At birth, each of us is amplified as an identical compounded twinning ratio of self in exact locations on Heaven and earth. We become an individual love frequency within the infinity sign that is the infinite grid of being love. A compound fraction of love is established at birth. The infinity symbol becomes an equation. It is another theory of relativity and a theory of loves reality. The equation of zero represents all-encompassing and eternal absolute love protection and automatically activates 'Unification of Everything.'"

On cue, Archangel Michael appeared standing next to Goddess. He smiled at me and continued where Jesus left off. "Please, for a moment close your eyes again and picture the number three hundred divided by twelve. 3+0+0=3 and 1+2=3. Both equations are three. When you add both answers to the equations together, 3+3=6, the answer is six. The number six is a compound, a bringing together to form a new whole, as a breakdown of the number three twice. Now I would like you to picture the number three hundred. The number three is direct to the left of two zeros. Pushing the two zeros together creates the infinity symbol, please push the infinity symbol to the left so it touches the indent of the number three. The number three and the infinity symbol now become a symbol on its own. This symbol represents, 'Infinite

A Catalyst

Creations of Love.' Please open your eyes. Megan, you like horses, don't you?"

"Yes," I replied.

"When a stallion is trained, a professional is necessary for the job. Do you agree?" asked Archangel Michael.

"Yes," I said.

"Please explain why," instructed Archangel Michael.

"If someone doesn't know how, they will be thrown off and get hurt," I responded.

Archangel Michael continued, "That is so. Your experience in Heaven I will describe in this way. The number three being the most significant as it applies to love. Number three is a group of love. The top line of the number three represents science and the 'Dialogue of Love.' The middle line represents music and 'Action of Love.' The bottom line represents math and 'Knowing Love.' The totality of the number three represents 'The Creation of All.' God is science, music, math, and 'The Creation of All.' Love is the number three riding you at a full gallop and has run you off the side of the Grand Canyon. Love is still connected to you at this moment. Your mind will immediately attach to the question why is this happening? As you fall faster, the question disappears because it doesn't matter. It is at this exact moment you will have surrendered. When you are falling toward the Colorado River, love has both trained you and structured you. It all happens twelve inches above the water. One plus two equals three. The number three is science, music, math, and 'The Creation of All.' Please stop me if you have any questions while I tell you this information. You are taking a large collection back for this book. I will continue. Goddess and Jesus have already explained to you the three seraphim. They are the 'Infinite Creations of Love.' Each was created by love's energy to assist with protecting love throughout the universes. Goddess informed you of the significant date of December 21st, 2012. December being the twelfth month, one plus two equals three. The twenty-first day is two plus one, again equaling the number three. The year two thousand twelve equals the number five representing the layer amounts in Heaven. When the three answers are added together, they equal the number eleven. Both ones represent perfect cohesion and are what you know as being the theory of relativity. The first one in the number eleven represents time. The second one in the number eleven represents space."

Goddess began, "It was Albert Einstein who introduced to the world the theory of relativity with E=mc2. His declaration of there being no time or space is partly correct. There is no definitive indication or representation of time. There is definitive space. Einstein also stated space-time as being part of a single fabric. Einstein continued explaining how each lengthens or contracts based upon energy from the person measuring them. Continuing with his theory, Einstein determined energy and matter as being aspects of the same object. He stated they could be converted into each other, E=mc2. E is energy, m is mass, and c is the speed of light. Einstein was noted for many things, but it is his theory of 'Mass-energy equivalence' you must mention with relation to 'Absolute Love Protection.' Einstein specified that if a body is stationary, it is internal energy he calls rest energy. Rest mass and rest energy are said to be equivalent and remain proportional to one another. Einstein also states when a body is in motion its total energy, or rest mass is an instrumental equation. Einstein

A Catalyst

believes each is the same because of the motion remaining the same. General relativity is considered to be extreme speeds or gravity, and each is referred to as an invariant mass. Nobody in motion can achieve the speed equivalent to that of rest mass. A body in motion does not have the endurance to reach the capabilities the mind is competent of achieving while in rest mass. Rest mass is also known as the power of thought. There is total energy, and rest mass acceleration being realized in the power of thought. Power of thought is the equivalent to the power of now. When this composition is used repetitiously, an alignment of all energies making up the human body produces a power of 'one.' No energy is more unrelenting than this form of the power of one. Repetitions at this magnitude are equivalent to cyclical energy. Cyclical energy is the most constant and contained energy."

Jesus picked up with ease, "Einstein stated $E=mc2$ can be used to indicate rest mass or (m or o), and rest energy (Eo) indicating their proportionality as, $Eo=moc2$. Etot, or simply E, is occasionally used to indicate the total energy and total mass of a moving body. The model, relativistic mass, is also called total mass. Total mass becomes noticeably greater when the speed of rest mass approaches to light. This is when special relativity is used to describe the motion. The totaling energy and totaling mass are stated as being the same as, $E=mrelc2$."

Archangel Michael began, "What has never been factored into Einstein's theory is a dialogue, the innate power of emotion. Emotion being 'energy in motion.' When a human is born, each enters the world with emotion. The emotion automatically dictates reactions from others around the child beginning at birth. The energy in motion begins at birth and is most powerful in this vulnerable state of being. Emotions in the birth

Megan C Brown

process are a complete existential statement. The birth of a newborn, like its heartbeat, has more energy than any other moving body used in creating Einstein's theory. The newborn is every absolute love. Each newborn is love, unconditional love, no judgment, pure energy, the highest frequency of love making all other love seem slow, constant circular speed encompassing entire universe, an endless washing of all frequencies comprising every soul the results include purification of all energies set forth from every other law, magnanimous supreme ruler, the soul of the outcome, mirror to all galaxies, the example of truth, displaying eternal love despite soul choices, and sole creator of endeavors that help build illusions."

Jesus continued, "A newborn baby is the most powerful frequency of love as he or she enters the world. The newborn is explaining the universe. At this moment, science, natural science, and philosophy of nature is being used simultaneously. This moment is when philosophy begins. A newborn is a physical state of energy making use of electrical energy. Childbirth is a performance of raw energy. The action of creation is being applied with absolute power. The absolute power of the birth performed is defined in physics as the force applied. Entering directly from the birth mother traveling from one state to another instantaneously changes the frequencies. The frequencies change automatically while leaving the birth mother to be entering the place of birth. A repetition of the birth process happens naturally. The birth process is a complete action of unseen energy containing the highest frequency of love in one location. Soul energy, chakra energy, and love energy. The birth cycle is invisible energy exercise always being a conduit to change."

A Catalyst

Goddess continued, "Following childbirth is the power of the mind, which is a learned process. Einstein stated total energy being the body in motion, as being greater than that of rest energy and equal to the laws of physics. The theory of relativity is extreme speeds of space and time. Einstein said total mass would become noticeably greater when the speed of rest mass approached the speed of light."

Jesus picked up, "Space-time has everything to do with being an intricate part of a single fabric. Space and time are woven into a single continuum known as space-time. This is the single fabric of energy having the ability to strengthen, lengthen, expand, and contract. Each can be achieved from the power of thought. Einstein was accurate in recognizing energy and matter as being the same object. Each one can be converted into the other. Einstein's theory of relativity being $E=mc2$ is an unfinished equation of parts. The equation will be complete when the chemical balance is factored into the 'Law of Science,' uniting with knowledge of energy having the capability to strengthen, lengthen, expand, and contract. Total mass cannot become greater until the understanding of what mass configuration is concerning one another is understood. The beginning amount of energy before any amount of energy is released must be removed from the configuration. Only then can the total loss be measured."

Archangel Michael continued, "A love frequency exists. The individual love frequency consists of matter within a central nucleus that is positively charged ions. It includes oxygen, deuterium, hydrogen, molecules, orbitals, photons, lithium, boron, and nitrogen. The mass state of an individual love frequency is a positive-positive

Megan C Brown

recipe. There is a recipe for love that exists, and science can prove it."

Goddess stated, "There is one 'Law of Science,' and it is superlative to all others. God and I are the one 'Law of Science.' Megan, have you heard the saying God is love?"

"Yes," I answered.

"God is love and so am I. God and I are science, music, and math. God is the creator of all," Goddess said.

Father Time "Love is a light no electrical current can ignite. Only a soul has the power to illuminate the brilliance of a flame so powerful. Bringing to life the power of love will change humanity's destiny."

Chapter 7
My love

It is with great ease I come to know love as my ruler. According to the laws of the universe, I have all the tools to turn a single mass that is a cell into a viral communion of love within. The cell morphology that is compounded in triplicate splays throughout all of me and awaits my daily acknowledgment to each as the gift each is to me. Once I have acknowledged them, it is as if I have permitted all cells to get to work inside of me. Bunches of love clusters will begin to accumulate by consciously visualizing love dots covering my body and connecting like neutrons sparking ignitions of light. This is my visualization approach to connecting to myself. Canonizing congruencies of definition within the fractionated compound brain frequencies. I have inhibited the nectar of love to prevail with my ability to once over the guidelines of my overall response with self, based upon an unbreakable energy force sequentially placed within the arch number code that is throughout the spherical embodiment of all that is me. What I am saying is for congruency of inner and outer places to link as the force fields, a salutation to self as one with the universe is mandatory. The linkage of self requires the knowledge of value in every other to bring the fluidity into the rigidity of loves dominance.

My entire life consists of variables I have chalked up to assignments of self; they are lengthy in my opinion because of my age. It does not matter the number of assignments. What matters is the base and foundation my body reacts. It all starts with the history of my mind already programmed as my character and way of being. How I choose to respond to my life condition depends on what is being triggered within me.

I bought a metaphorical car called love. As the driver, I am the speedometer. My mental love vehicle is also made from a triple compounded love frequency that makes up the entire frame, body, paint, wheels, and everything else. My energetic input determines how powerful the acceleration of love will be. I determine how the engine will perform, how fast I will go, and what the speed limit of every moment is going to be. The greatest part is, knowing my love has no restrictions.

Getting back to my fluency of love, it is not an egocentric mental state of being I have described using my love vehicle metaphor as the proverbial example. Instead, I am introducing another avenue that opened to find out about myself, but I had to walk the new block. In Heaven, I am perfect in all ways, just as everyone else is.

I must look at myself as being a Second Holy Trinity. The Father, the Son, and the Holy Spirit. The Father is my mind, the Son is my communicator, and the Holy Spirit is my soul. The way I need to think must include the Creator by any given name. Whether it be God, Supreme Ruler, Allah, Abba, Prophet Muhammad, Adonai, ha Shem, Creator, Elohim, Yahweh, Jesus, Almighty, El, Jehovah, Messiah, Alpha and Omega, Yeshua, King of Kings, El-

A Catalyst

Shaddai, God Himself, Shandi, Zhu, humanism, Shen, Tian, Tanri, Hu, and Parvardigar. God sent Prophet Muhammad and Jesus to be His communicator. I remember while I was sitting in a Catholic mass listening to the priest talks about the Holy Trinity. It was said that God is all three. He is, but there is more than One Holy Trinity. There is a Second Holy Trinity; I am human therefore I am the reflection of the First Holy Trinity in living, walking form. A reflection makes me the Second Holy Trinity. People wonder what God looks like. I have seen Him in Heaven, and He is beautiful! God is on earth too in every person I see. Because each soul is a creation of God, it automatically makes every one of us the Second Holy Trinity. We do not have to see God's face in Heaven to uncover the mystery of life. We must love everyone as being the reflection of God that each of us is on earth. We are each a mystery of life.

How does the Second Holy Trinity fall into my life outside of church? My metaphorical car drives forward with instructions and mindfulness of staying in the moment. Be in the now.

Stonehenge mapped much of the Neanderthal, a new species of human ancestor. Stonehenge revealed the ancient Mayan city of Caracal, now in Belize. There were three long bone fragments with DNA linking together three different female Neanderthals in Croatia about 38,000-45,000 years ago. There was a finding of human DNA having bred with the Neanderthals. Approximately 1-4% of the hereditary are in Eurasia and were derived from Neanderthals. The Neanderthals are closely related to all non-Africans. It is speculated the actual genetic mixture happened in the Middle East after humans left Africa. There were seventy-eight amino acid differences found between Neanderthals and humans. It is said

63

Megan C Brown

Neanderthal samples have the ancestral state, and human samples have an evolutionary state. Using Stonehenge's findings as my example, all of us are a mixture of celestial beings with our ancestral beginnings on earth in Africa according to God Himself.

What is my point in veering so far left of center in my explanation of love? In my opinion, we are all a bit left or right of center. If we would all practice the love ritual with self it would keep us centered. Do I have proof of what I am writing? Yes, all of it is written in Heaven. Many millenniums have become a part of history to humanity. Every soul survived and thrived by the power of love but did not know it.

Getting back to the knowledge of value in everyone to bring forth the fluidity into the rigidity of love's dominance, begins with self. I must love myself to continue to stay on course in my everyday life. Whether I choose to be ancestral, evolutionary, or just plain celestial does not matter. What matters is how I honor myself as being the Second Holy Trinity. I have an obligation to God and Heaven to keep myself balanced with love from within, so the teetering of uncertainty is eradicated. It is a daily job, and I am the only one who can do it. What is real is the difference of an ever-changing world in which we live as a united force of energy linking us to a cosmic force that is love. Then I ask myself, am I linked to me?

Chapter 8
Where Is the Love?

There was a time when the mental scramble included the words, 'Oh my God. What do I do now?' Here is the kicker. The words have on occasion still surfaced.

What do I do now to respond differently? I meditate. Why is meditation so important to me? It helps me stay in the driver's seat of my love vehicle in every way. I don't sit down and try to think of anything. I talk to God, Goddess, Jesus, Prophet Muhammad, Archangel Michael, and Gaius Julius Caesar just to name some of them. I like to discuss as the narrator what it is, I'm dealing with at any given time, and let it all out. Do I expect a response? Yes. I spoke of how we have linked ancestrally, evolutionarily, and celestially so therefore I have no doubt I am connected. Getting beyond my connection to those I choose to speak to in Heaven, I talk about everything. Why not, they see everything and then replay it for me when it is time to return to Heaven. How do they answer me? It's interesting to feel a responsibility to myself come into my mind. Is it God, I don't know? It sounds like me answering myself, and I didn't know the feeling or answer before I sat down to meditate. I do believe I am receiving a response from Heaven.

Meditation means long or deep thinking about spiritual matters, I liken everything to being spiritual in thought now. However, spiritual means not composed of matter. The mind is a matter. A mind thinks about a major object of interest or concern on a moment-to-moment basis. If the mind did not, how would a human function? When I sit and think it is the amount of energy in my mind, I give toward any one topic that creates the matter, but spiritual to me suggests not giving the matter too much energy so as not to be thrown off-center. It all comes down to balance within. The saying mind over matter has become the fractionated compound brain theory for me. Remembering when I sit down the common denominator is always three hundred, but the numerator I can control, and I need it to be zero. The only way to be zero is to accept all that is happening in my life. I did not say like all that is happening to me. I am saying I must agree to receive whether willingly or reluctantly everything I am involved in that I cannot walk away from. I must also agree to receive willingly or reluctantly who I am. This makes the fractionated compound brain theory compounded twofold.

The fractionated compound brain theory is a creation by Hippocrates, but for those who do not believe I have had any connection at all with Heaven, I created the fractionated compound brain theory. In any case, it is worth thinking about. Imagine an arch that covers every thought being a fraction. The fraction is a two-piece equation at the end of my meditation equaling one answer. Physical energy is divided by psychological equaling the individual outcome. The physical energy I put into every moment divided by my mind matter

A Catalyst

equaling the numerator that is over the constant common denominator being three hundred.

The three hundred compound is enough on its own to grasp admittedly, but there is more I haven't spoken of on these pages yet. The ratio of compounding a moment-by-moment love frequency seems a bit of a stretch. So much work, it keeps me in check to always be in the moment of serenity. The word indicates not being loud in pitch or volume. Yes, a volume in my mind. It correlates with the energy I give to any circumstance. My volume and pitch are really about the amount of energy, levels of energy if you will. Am I ambushing myself, or am I softening therefore relinquishing the power of the situation at hand? It sounds beautiful when I think about it this way. I have the power to soften the blow with the love of self-rudimentary in every way. The birth cycle enhances and finalizes the early level characteristic of the beginning skill and development of self. I am a self-source of love by way of my birth cycle as is everyone else. Knowing about this moment that includes a bunch of laws of the universe helps me to understand where I need to be when I sit or lie down to meditate. Talking to souls in Heaven or simply visualizing a golden rose and watching it unfold to take me to a centered place within does not matter. What matters is that I get to silence myself within. No mind chatters, solace.

Just for fun, I do the meditation. It lifts me from within as if I've released exercised endorphins I have. I am not a doctor, but something wonderful is happening when I exercise in this manner. There is a distinct body inside of my physical body formed by the combining of two or more different things within myself, the physical and psychological division problem. Having stated the physical and psychological being divided by one another

Megan C Brown

seems incongruent with reality. Reality is also multi-dimensional, and this must continue to be viewed by scientists as a reality. Multi-dimensional is not just a bunch of Twilight Zone episodes. It just has yet to be figured out to the full extent that it is. Man has traveled to the moon. What dimension is that? I would guess a fifth dimension like the Twilight Zone, as mentioned in the opening credits of the television show.

Rod Serling was way ahead of his time. Blessings received for the anecdote to self, Mr. Serling. It was you who introduced to the world a way of thinking that was outside of commonplace dialogue with one another. I continue to lift my metaphorical candle to you and your brilliance. Now my hope for a continued movement forward to the understanding of the fifth dimension is to introduce the seventh dimension. I have read a network executive asked the writer why a fifth dimension had not been mentioned. Rod Serling was said to have been puzzled and replied, "Oh, aren't there five?" The narration was re-recorded.

The ever-changing variables to keep us from seeing the rest of the sixth dimension have to do with energy input.

It was Albert Einstein, like Life and Dimensions on Earth – Part ½, courtesy of Linda Dillon, Council of Love, who said, "Humans usually think of dimensions in terms of measurement. The term "measurement" refers to the length, width, depth in the third dimension, with the added element of time is the fourth; and numeric assignment to the fifth. I wish you, my dear friends, to think of dimensions differently, not excluding measurement but as a measurement of growth and qualities of being states of existence. As humans, you have come to consider growth as the core definition of

A Catalyst

what is alive: what is living. Examples of this would be trees, plants, animals, crystals, and of course human beings. It is natural for you to think of yourselves as the top rung of the food chain of life which expresses in the third dimension.

What you and I, when in form, failed to realize is that life, life forms, and dimensions are not a ladder but rather a circle. That circle of 12 dimensions, each with 12 planes, defines this universe in which all life forms participate, or have the capacity to participate.

Each dimension has qualities, or growth patterns, that define it. That is the concept of dimensional measurement; you are measuring the energy force of that quality. Each of these dimensions has its significance as it were, and of course, within this, there is a gradation, much the same way as a diamond has a gradation. I wish to discuss these but first I outline them.

But before I do, it is necessary to put your preconceptions and judgments about ascendancy aside. Each dimension has a plethora of gifts or learning opportunities, opportunities for evolution on the physical and spiritual scale. What you also must need to realize is that all these dimensions operate and are observable in the third dimension.

One of the qualities of the third dimension is the ability to observe all dimensions and realities in the physical life form. Now it is time to pay attention to what is being represented to you but that you have not adequately observed. I suggest this to you because that is part of the process of being born into the third dimension; it is the possibility and the responsibility to observe like a scientist.

The first dimension is amorphous, having no defined or classified form. Believe it or not, ideas fall into this categorization. Ideas are simply chemical electromagnetic events. Ideas have no form until they are brought into action and form. You have an experience of this dimension when you are brainstorming or free-associating, letting ideas move and circulate throughout the inter-dimensional field. That is why so often there are similar concepts or scientific discoveries at the same time. It is from this place that the understanding of the 100th monkey emerges. Both the first and second dimensions hold the qualities of humility and prudence.

The second dimension has the aspect of flat spatial extent, meaning that there is no depth and therefore often not perceived by the human eyes. The quality of this dimension is the ability to mutate, grow and evolve from one amorphous mass into another and so on. These are often micro-organisms, viruses, or bacteria, such as a common cold. Cancer also falls into this dimension, evolving from a cell and often mutating into a tumor or growth. Usually, the life form of the first dimension is only observable under a microscope, but the presence of this life form is evidenced both in nature and within your physical bodies. This dimension teaches inter-dependence as life forms are dependent upon a host whether it is a human form, air, water, and so on.

Many life forms inhabit this universe who are of this nature, popping in and out depending on whether they are facing you or not. Not many of them inhabit your planet, but one example is of the Serros (1) who feed energetically upon humans. This is not a malign activity, but simply an inter-dependence that one life form must attach to another to survive. The quality of this lifeform, like the first, is that there is no experience of emotion. It is learning to simply be in form and learn interdependence without the presence of emotion.

A Catalyst

What many of the scientists are defining in String Theory as the other eleven dimensions are in fact aspects of the twelve planes of this dimension. They have not yet made the quantum leap to understanding that dimensions are not defined by physicality but by qualities of growth.

The third dimension as you are aware is defined by the quality of the perception or experience of physicality, meaning that the universe is perceived through the experience of length, width, depth. But the growth quality is the ability to embrace all dimensions, realities, emotions, and spirit. It also has the unique quality of freedom of choice. All the numerically higher dimensions can exhibit in the third. The growth opportunity and quality of the third is the ability to choose to expand beyond the mere perception of physicality and incorporate all aspects of self.

This is what the Universal Mother (2) talks about when she is discussing incorporating all aspects of self. The third dimension is not limited by the time-space continuum; it merely appears to be. That is the challenge and the opportunity in the third is to reach beyond physical appearances.

The fourth dimension is the quality of magic, which many of you think of as alchemy. (3) It is the growth into the realization and action of being an agent for transformation, transmutation, and transubstantiation. This dimension is very easily accessible from your third and is witnessed continually by living masters such as Sai Baba; divas; fairies, elementals, and so on. You need to realize that once you have anchored this growth component within yourself, i.e., once you have anchored the fourth dimension lessons and growth within your being, these beings and abilities will be not only visible

71

but commonplace. An everyday human example of this dimension, and one which bothered me throughout my human life, was the splitting of the atom. What you think of as science is often simply operating within this dimension.

The fifth dimension of growth opportunity is the ability to cope, create, manage, and manipulate change. This channel has often spoken of the fifth dimension where the quality of change is constant. That is correct but the rationale behind this is that the being is learning how to deal with and create change. It is the precursor to creation. You live in an infinite universe, one that is constantly in the process of change and growth. If you are not able to manage change internally and externally then you cannot incorporate the qualities of the higher dimensions with grace. Therefore, the growth aspect of the fifth is the ability to move through change, manipulating it in ways that are loving, kind, considerate of self and the collective, and respectful of the grander plan of unfoldment.

There has been a great deal of discussion about the Earth, Terra Gaia, moving into the fifth dimension. This speaks to a fundamental misunderstanding of the quality of dimensions. The dimensions are not fixed points on a compass, they are a circle dancing, moving and expanding constantly. There is constant movement with and between all the dimensions – they are fluid. The plant, animal, and human kingdoms collectively have been intensely learning the lessons of constant change.

What do you think the explosion in technology, human advances, and thinking has been about? The human community has managed enormous change in the past few hundred years. No, not always well or wisely but that is the nature of the dimension; it offers the

A Catalyst

opportunity to learn the growth lessons of that dimension. Gaia, which operates at a very different frequency and time/space continuum from humans, has conquered the lessons of change eons ago. So have most of the other kingdoms.

So, when there is the discussion about moving from one dimension to another, simply think of it as moving from one classroom to another, passing from one grade to another, all while understanding that sometimes you have to go back and review basic principles to remind yourself what you learned and forgot. You do not eliminate the spatial and time continuum because you are moving inter-dimensionally. You are expanding yourself while remaining in the form and expression of the third dimension.

The qualities of growth that occur as part of the shifting in and through the fifth dimension are patience, stamina, humor, and wisdom that the more things change the more they are constant. Love and joy are constants, my friend. And by the way, why would you think these blessings and qualities are the exclusive purviews of the third dimension-that is true of the human ego.

When he spoke of the sixth dimension, he said it was his favorite. "It is the place or state of being where ideas and belief systems mutate into form. This dimension has often been identified by this channel as the dimension of chaos. There are many above and below who would suggest that humanity collectively is in the process of experiencing the growth opportunities of the sixth. When we say chaos, we speak of it in terms of creative chaos, for in every chaotic situation, whether it is internal such as cancer or external such as war or societal breakdown, there is an opportunity for growth. Often you have heard me speak of the process of implosion/explosion of creation. Chaos is the nucleus for that action and outcome. It can be beautiful and magnificent. Think of it as the Big Bang, think of it as the birth of a solar system, the death of a star. The biggest opportunity for growth of the sixth dimension is the understanding that you are not in control. It brings with it the growth of the qualities of surrender, trust, fortitude, and hope. It is the ability to acknowledge that seemingly random chaos has a Divine patterning. It teaches the lessons of reaping what you sow. It brings forth a profound appreciation of the gift of the unknown."

Stepping into a new thought for a moment, I would like to discuss the seventh dimension. No one has talked about the central part or aspect of every human, the soul. What is it? According to the dictionary, the soul is an immaterial force within a human being thought to give the body life, energy, and power. The soul is an energy that gives animation to living beings. What this means is humanity could not exist without the energy of the soul according to Heaven. Why will I incorporate Heaven as fact? Because I have been there. God, Goddess, Jesus, Prophet Muhammad, Julius Caesar, and Hippocrates are a lot smarter than me.

So, what is it that I am proposing with a seventh dimension? The ability to construct self with the power of thought using Albert Einstein's thought process, "…growth of the qualities of surrender, trust, fortitude, and hope. It is the ability to acknowledge that seemingly random chaos has a Divine patterning. It teaches the lessons of reaping what you sow. It brings forth a profound appreciation of the gift of the unknown." A seventh dimension is a connection to myself, my soul, with my mind asking for love to fill my body and construct new cells throughout my entire body to heal

A Catalyst

and reconstruct the current foundation of my physical self. By asking my soul directly I am talking to my origin with trust, fortitude, and hope. I am canceling out chaos and surrender with knowing what it is I want. I will be exhibiting another form of Divine patterning. In doing this I will bring forth a profound appreciation of a gift that is known because I am claiming it with exactness. I am telling my body how to behave.

As Albert Einstein once said, "Ethical axioms are found and tested not very differently from the axioms of science. Truth is what stands the test of experience." Or Arthur Schopenhauer said, "All truth passes through three stages. First, it is ridiculed. Second, it is violently opposed. Third, it is accepted as being self-evident."

I have discussed my layman version of energy input, but there is more. The frequency speed in everybody that currently covers the moon is at a much higher rate. We cannot see a faster speed of a human form without being able to achieve a faster cylindrical speed in ourselves. If I do not match the invisible variable, or am likely to change frequently, suddenly, or unexpectedly with whom I am trying to connect, it will be impossible to be static without an even keel or consistency. Consistency is the key to exchange frequencies of this caliber, there can be no dip. It must be maintained at a certain number and rise from there for clarity of definition to be seen.

The Romans built the timeless piece called the Coliseum amphitheater. Anyone to have conceived such a vision as the Roman Coliseum had to have united with a profound force of nature from within. Until the Roman Empire, there was no greater display of furthering conditions of the mind. To have grasped the cognition of relativity lacking Albert Einstein's formulation for the theory of relativity, suggests an innate character that is

Megan C Brown

housed within the confines of our minds. Having suggested the theory of relativity before its actual creation sounds absurd. What is absurd is to illicit a period as being without the necessary tools to perform as the geniuses each of us is. Not including the entirety of every soul, would be remissive of the point that I have been ordered by God to make somehow.

Many generations of lives have been and continue to be shaped by extraordinary behavior displays throughout our existence. Because of consistency inside of the structures, that is the entire foundation that is our lives, a union being love can never be understood as being the human archetype. As I will discuss within the coming pages the ease with which a soul falls effortlessly through the societal glass ceiling constructed around the dome that is one's mind can never be shattered. Until our minds are without consuming what appears to be a reality as our life, all of humanity can never part the non-existent. Collective, innate, patterns mean every idea in everyone's psyche is an attribute from the originator of all that is. Which brings me back to love; where is the love? This perplexing question became aligned one day while I was driving my son home from school. A song by the same name played on the radio and for whatever reason engaged my concentration on a single thought. It was in that moment I understood the wherewithal of every one of my life tragedies as being my conductor throughout my life's course. So, while I situate myself throughout my life's puzzle pieces, I have ever so carefully carried in my energy field, I must purposely situate my mind in a thought pattern of love, why? I did not comprehend my power that is God-given, and it applies to everyone. Whether or not I recognize a ruler that is God, a ruler that is a tree, a ruler that is a bug, a ruler that is a peace sign,

A Catalyst

or a ruler that is a permanent fixture inside of my mind there is only one magnanimous ruler of all that is, love. At what time does everyone begin to apply the timelessness origin of all that is a most superior vision of hope? Until applications of love are every band-aid for every wound, every person covering the entire globe with a purposeful charged comprehension of self will inevitably be without direction for a journey within. Going within is a soul's innate course for achieving the recognition it deeply yearns for an entire existence.

Where does the seventh dimension come in with all I have just splayed out? The seventh dimension is my soul. How can a seventh dimension exist?

The first, second, third, fourth, fifth, and sixth dimensions are each a makeup of the human form. The seventh dimension is a way of thinking. It is this simple, the life force within stems from my soul: my soul is pure love.

Wolfgang Amadeus Mozart "Neither a lofty degree of intelligence nor imagination nor both together go to the making of genius. Love, love, love, that is the soul of genius."

Chapter 9
The Star of David Defined

Whosoever shall be tending to adhere to the life force of God as thy ruler must first look to the Star of David. This symbol is the triumphant force behind liberty and justice for all. The conquering of an elemental illness called hate, deprivation, and segregation must happen for unity to thrive. There is no reason other than human ignorance, laziness, and complacency for our current global stagnation to peace. There are more reasons, but I feel those three apply to most of humanity. It may seem pompous to have made this statement, but I feel it's pompous to ignore reality.

The nations covering our globe are run in conformity to that which dominates and governs the societal belief systems. It is we the people in the United States of America who are obligated as citizens to demand:

"The unanimous Declaration of the thirteen united States of America, when in the course of human events, it becomes necessary for one people to dissolve the political bands which have connected them with another, and to assume among the powers of the earth, the separate and equal station to which the Laws of Nature and Nature's

Megan C Brown

God entitle them, a decent respect to the opinions of mankind requires that they should declare the causes which impel them to the separation. We hold these truths to be self-evident, that all men are created equal, that they are endowed by their Creator with certain unalienable rights, that among these are life, liberty, and the pursuit of happiness. That to secure these rights, governments are instituted among men deriving their just powers from the consent of the governed, that whenever any Form of Government becomes destructive of these ends, it is the right of the People to alter or to abolish it, and to institute new government, laying its foundation on such principles and organizing its powers in such form, as to them shall seem most likely to affect their safety and happiness. Prudence, indeed, will dictate that governments long established should not be changed for light and transient causes; and accordingly, all experience hath shown, that mankind is more disposed to suffer, while evils are sufferable than to right themselves by abolishing the forms to which they are accustomed. But when a long train of abuses and usurpations, pursuing invariably the same object evinces a design to reduce them under absolute despotism, it is their right, it is their duty, to throw off such Government, and to provide new guards for their future security—Such has been the patient sufferance of these colonies, and such is now the necessity which constrains them to alter their former systems of government. The history of the present King of Great Britain is a history of repeated injuries and usurpations, all having in direct object the establishment of an absolute tyranny of these states. To prove this, let facts be submitted to a candid world. He has refused his assent to laws, the most wholesome and necessary for the public good. He has forbidden his governors to pass laws of

A Catalyst

immediate and pressing importance unless suspended in their operation till his assent should be obtained; and when so suspended, he has utterly neglected to attend to them. He has refused to pass other laws for the accommodation of large districts of people unless those people would relinquish the right of representation in the legislature; a right is inestimable to them and formidable to tyrants only. He has called together legislative bodies at places unusual, uncomfortable, and distant from the depository of their public records, for the sole purpose of fatiguing them into compliance with his measures. He has dissolved representative houses repeatedly, for opposing with manly firmness his invasions on the rights of the people. He has refused for a long time, after such dissolutions, to cause others to be elected; whereby the legislative powers, incapable of annihilation, have returned to the People at large for their exercise; the state remaining in the meantime exposed to all the dangers of invasion from without, and convulsions within. He has endeavored to prevent the population of these states; for that purpose, obstructing the laws for naturalization of foreigners; refusing to pass others to encourage their migrations hither, and raising the conditions of new appropriations of lands.

He has obstructed the administration of justice, by refusing his assent to laws for establishing judiciary powers. He has made judges dependent on his will alone, for the tenure of their offices, and the amount and payment of their salaries. He has erected a multitude of new offices and sent hither swarms of officers to harass our people and ear out their substance. He has kept among us, in times of peace, standing armies without the consent of our legislatures. He has affected to render the military independent of and superior to the civil power.

Megan C Brown

He has combined with others to subject us to a
jurisdiction foreign to our constitution, and
unacknowledged by our laws, giving his assent to their
acts of pretended legislation: For quartering large bodies
of armed troops among us: For protecting them, by a
mock trial, from punishment for any murders which they
should commit on the inhabitants of these states: For
cutting off our trade with all parts of the world: For
imposing taxes on us without our consent: For depriving
us in many cases, of the benefits of trial by jury: For
transporting us beyond seas to be tried for pretended
offenses: For abolishing the free system of English laws in
a neighboring province, establishing therein arbitrary
government, and enlarging its boundaries to render it at
once an example and fit instrument for introducing the
same absolute rule into these colonies: For taking away
our charters, abolishing our most valuable laws, and
altering fundamentally the forms of our governments:
For suspending our legislatures and declaring themselves
invested with power to legislate for us in all cases
whatsoever. He has abdicated government here, by
declaring us out of his protection and waging war against
us. He has plundered our seas, ravaged our coasts, burnt
us towns, and destroyed the lives of our people. He is
currently transporting large armies of foreign
mercenaries to complete the works of death, desolation,
and tyranny, already begun with circumstances of cruelty
& perfidy scarcely paralleled in the most barbarous ages,
and unworthy the head of a civilized nation. He has
constrained our fellow citizens taken captive on the high
seas to bear arms against their country, to become the
executioners of their friends and brethren, or to fall
themselves by their hands. He has excited domestic
insurrections amongst us and has endeavored to bring on

A Catalyst

the inhabitants of our frontiers, the merciless Indian savages, whose known rule of warfare, is an undistinguished destruction of all ages, sexes, and conditions." (U.S. National Archives and Records Administration, 2022)

I thought back to when I was sitting next to Bach, and Mozart at the golden table in Temple where they had each been ordered by God to explain the reality of life to me. They began informing me about the exactness of Latin. Latin was the only language at the beginning of time. The conflict began to arise two thousand years after the creation of the earth. The original three continents experienced dissemination of difference within their own cultures. Another language was created as protection. Italian was the first form of code talking. Mozart explained music as being a love frequency at 528 Hz. Using Latin as an example, there are thousands of languages now extinct.

I began to think for a moment about extinctions occurring throughout our world of languages, cultures, people, occupations, and spiritual education. Extinctions are occurring, and no one is paying attention. A deafening reality is repeating, and gradually reducing the difference. Bach pointed out the nonexistent currencies in Europe; creating sameness through currency is one way of dismissing differences within humanity. There is an uncaring reality flourishing in our daily reality. Primary languages along with tribes, cultures, spirituality, personal interests, and unconditional love are becoming extinct. Money is being used as one of the definitions of, success, and viewed in Heaven as prevailing blindness. The riches and abundance of love each of our souls brings to life are more powerful than any dollar amount could ever be. Mozart shared with me how family, friendships, and celebratory gatherings filled love from within. Individuals once thrived mentally knowing they were loved.

Mozart hopes music appreciation classes will become mandatory for every school student throughout the world, penetrating students with musical, emotional, and psychological interpretations of his music love frequency. These classes could be a new equalizer for humanity. He hopes this form of enlightenment will be introduced starting in pre-school and continue throughout high school and college. Mozart declared, "This music frequency has no language barrier!"

Mozart went on to explain a unification of two specific musical notes. One is 'b' triple sharp, and the other is 'c' triple sharp. A triple sharp means each of these notes are played as a sharp. All three 'c' sharps and all three 'b' sharps played simultaneously. When all three octaves of each note are played simultaneously, a metaphorical gateway opens a direct connection to a LOVEPATH. The ability to open this LOVEPATH can only be achieved on piano or keyboard. Those who play the notes daily will open a direct link to love's messages. The LOVEPATH is the highest frequency of love; your soul will be ignited automatically as a result of playing the three octaves of the two notes simultaneously. Each soul is programmed at the time of its conception to respond. The individual soul will receive the appropriate information from the love it needs at that moment. Like a muscle, the more often these notes are played the outcome will always be a stronger soul connection to its creator, Love.

When Mozart finished explaining to me the ways of unlocking love for healing, he quietly looked down at the table, a formal character of him surfaced. Mozart's

A Catalyst

excitement was gone as he looked back up at me with a serious look on his face. He said, "Priorities of a person's life are to consist of love. Achieving appreciation of one's soul-self is paramount in understanding the value of sameness. When I composed my music, I had hoped every individual would tap into a deeper understanding of self. Love is the universal objective. This paycheck will never change."

Bach said, "If I could superimpose every composition, I have created with my eternal knowing, each composite would catapult a more advanced love frequency. This love frequency would speak a universal language. The totality of this love frequency would ricochet throughout the world, causing soul expansions in love."

Mozart looked at me and asked, "Do you know your soul mission, Megan?"

The surprise must have been my facial expression when Mozart asked me such a purposeful question. I was still pondering school children learning of a love frequency in music class, currencies in our world-changing, soul expansions in love, and acceptance being equal to love. My inability to respond was not because I did not want to; I did not know what to say. So, when asked if I knew what my soul mission was, not even a thought bubble existed. My mind was twirling with the fact I was included in a cerebral discussion regarding music frequencies with two of the greatest composers in music history! What could I say?

Both received my silence as the unawareness it was, and thankfully neither of them took offense. Bach gently asked me, "Would you like to share with us what you are knowing in this now?"

Megan C Brown

"Yes, every message of peace displayed throughout world history has resulted in resistance. Every time peace is introduced, it is met with a resistance to change," I replied respectfully.

"That is so," Mozart said. "Please ask us any questions you may have. We are both here to assist you."

I was encouraged by Mozart's sincerity. I continued to speak gently and ask questions. Each continued as my counselor until I understood everything. Unexpectedly, God appeared in His chair at the head of His table. We stood immediately and bowed.

God began, "Please be seated, I am here to comfort you. Your soul capabilities are much greater than you realize. Come stand before Me."

I walked away from my chair and stood before God as He requested. I bowed my head and said, "Yes, Your Holiness. I am at Your service."

God informed me, "I am always with you."

I smiled at God. "Please forgive me. My intentions are good, but I still need help in letting go of fear," I answered.

God answered me with a question. "What do you fear? This has been your home before, we don't bite." He smiled at me.

I laughed at His response.

God continued, "Oh good, you remember. Let Me remind you, your soul never dies. How your soul lives after death is ultimately your decision. Peace and happiness are always available for you here. This has been your toughest life. You can do it," God said comfortingly. The room felt still and full at the same time.

Instinctively, at this moment, I lifted my arms and tilted my head back to look up at the ceiling. With God's eyes only, He infused my entire being. When I say God

A Catalyst

infused me with the Star of David, it might sound strange, but it has come to make perfect sense to me. God is Jewish and so is everyone in His congregation. As it turns out, there is a science that is specific to the Star of David. In no way am I desecrating Judaism. I intend to give understanding to the sacred Star of David.

Thousands of years ago, the Star of David was amiss, but reintroduced to King David by God and Archangel Michael. It was the reintroduction to King David by the powerful apparition that made the Star of David known to humanity again.

To further assist Judaism, every religious faith should know that Archangel Michael, according to the Book of Enoch, is the prince of Israel. Each point of the Star of David is currently a mystery. I will start at the top point and move clockwise in the explanation given to me by King David. The first point represents love. The second point represents Heaven. The third point represents humanity. The fourth and bottom point represents love. The fifth point represents food. The sixth point represents health. Beginning at the top again the first point represents earth. The second point represents fire. The third point represents water. The fourth and bottom point represents air. The fifth point represents metal. The sixth point represents love. So, what is with the two different meanings for each point of this sacred Star of David? It simply means there is love above us and below us. The intricate version is this: First, there is love that covers our earth. The second point is Heaven, being the highest frequency of love, is over the fire or ignition of love. The third point is representative of humans are made up of water. The fourth point is air is the constant mover of love. The fifth point is the coagulation of metal in the body and everything that nourishes us. The sixth

Megan C Brown

point is love rules our health. There is a third layer to the Star of David. The first point is God who is a creation of love. The second point is Archangel Gabriel who is in Heaven and represents fire. The third point is Archangel Michael who is the protector of humanity and represents water. The fourth point is Archangel Michael who is also love's creation and he represents air. The fifth point is Moses who represents food and metal. The sixth point is Melchizedek who is the body of love representing health. It was Melchizedek who wrote Tikkun Olam which means 'world repair.' Tikkun Olam means 'social action' and the pursuit of 'social justice.' The origin of this phrase is in classical rabbinic literature and a major strand of Jewish mysticism beginning with the work of a kabbalist named Isaac Luria in the 16th century. The Star of David is the symbol of love.

There is another religion called Islam created by Prophet Muhammad (May the peace and blessings of God be upon Him), who was also seated at God's golden table in the Temple. Why would the example of Islam be seated with a congregation ruled by Judaism? Because He is also a representative of Judaism. This is not a joke! While He was the Prophet in his life on earth and still is in Heaven, He adheres to the Judaic understanding of the Star of David and what it means. The word Islam means voluntary "submission" or "surrender" to the will of God. The word Islam is from the root word "salaam" meaning peace. This is absolute: Muslims are peaceful people.

The beautiful point I want to make for Islam is that it was Prophet Muhammad who received an apparition from God. It was Prophet Muhammad who wrote the Quran by God's orders, just as King David wrote much of the Torah. The Quran is the very word of God almighty.

A Catalyst

The star and crescent are the symbols representing Intergalactic Love. This explanation I am writing I do with love. It was Prophet Muhammad who ordered me to make certain things known. With absolute respect for Islam, the Quran, and Prophet Muhammad I will continue my explanations. The star and crescent represent the multiple galaxies, moons, and planets. The star represents every star Intergalactically. Just as the Star of David represents love, so too does the star and crescent. Please refer to the Star of David points and note it is Heaven and earth. The star and crescent are every galaxy and star, both symbols represent love. Green is most sacred to Islam according to Prophet Muhammad. Green also symbolizes life and nature according to Prophet Muhammad.

There is a universal agreement that I have created since my near-death experience. It was inspired by God, Goddess, Jesus, Prophet Muhammad, King David, Quan Yin, Buddha, Sitting Bull, White Eagle, Archangel Michael, Archangel Gabriel, Julius Caesar, Joan of Arc, and every Angel, Archangel, saint, and ascended master I met in Heaven.

Our globe will be run in conformity to that which dominates and governs the societal belief systems. Love, peace, and happiness to everyone. It is we the people on earth who are obligated as citizens to demand, during human events, it becomes necessary for humanity to unite with one another despite personal religious belief systems harming no one. Every individual is separate and equal by soul laws. The Laws of Nature and Nature's God entitle every law-abiding citizen due respect.

"We hold these truths to be self-evident, that all are created equal, that they are endowed by their Creator with certain unalienable Rights, that among these are

Megan C Brown

Life, Liberty, and the pursuit of Happiness. That whenever any Form of Government becomes destructive of these ends, it is the Right of the People to alter or to abolish it, and to institute new Government, laying its foundation on such principles and organizing its powers in such form, as to them shall seem most likely to affect their safety and happiness. But when a long train of abuses and usurpations, pursuing invariably the same object evinces a design to reduce them under absolute despotism, it is their right, it is their duty, to throw off such government, and to provide new guards for their future security. Such has been the patient sufferance of our globe, and such is now the necessity that constrains the world to alter their former systems of government, the history is a history of repeated injuries and usurpations. To prove this, let facts be submitted to a candid world. Additionally, let us uniform our globe with the universal declaration of human rights, and the declaration on the rights of the child." (U.S. National Archives and Records Administration, 2022)

Chapter 10
Surrendering to Grow

My life has been a plethora of experiences as expected in my age bracket. What has surfaced are many situations where I have been tested by the universe as to how I will respond. It has not always been easy, but I get through just like the rest of the world, one day at a time.

I began to think of my life as my favorite baseball team. What do these stellar players have that makes them the shining stars in their league? Seriously, what does it take for them to enter the major league and stay there? A multitude of things in my opinion, but it's the mental stamina and consistent commitment both physically and mentally. Each player must condition themselves individually, as well as with the team they play with to keep playing with the team; the strategic mind working in unison with others and making it seem so fluid and effortless. It took the players years of commitment of practice and self-conditioning. The gift each of them displays as they slide into base, or throw the perfect pitch is quite remarkable. I think of baseball as meditation. The exactness of every move is truly being in the moment. It's awesome! Garrett Morris in Saturday Night Live as Chico Escuela said it best, 'Baseball's been berry good to me.'

I have been to a few baseball games, and every time I zone in on what is happening. I watch everything and get into my Zen experience. I love it. My life's tough times are self-conditioning of another sort. I'm running my metaphorical bases and hitting home runs of another kind.

Life is a baseball game to me. I'm the batter every day in my life running the bases, and alert to the other players participating in my outcome. I am not going to soften or minimize my life saying it reminds me of the very skilled game of baseball. I am suggesting life can be watched from another seat. The one that is level right behind home plate is where I start, but it is best to watch from a bit higher up to the same location. The view of everyone is a bit different and great. When I can see and feel everything as the players are running bases, I won't miss the motion of the players as they move in front of one another. So where am I going with baseball and me? I liken my first, second, third bases, and home plate to be my daily thoughts. Will I run them all in and bring my action to fruition? I have the choice; how will I participate in my life?

To each his own, I say. How I align myself in my everyday life is what it comes down to. The comfort of knowing the strategy of my day can be changed in a moment is wonderful. It's all about the glass being half full.

I oversee how I internalize my day and to some degree my life daily. What a concept! I think about my life daily. So, what do I think? It depends on the day. Some days are easy for me to fall in line with, and sometimes I wish I was not experiencing my life as it is in the moment.

A Catalyst

I must separate from the moment and put it in perspective. What do I mean? I put effort into my everyday process, and I have accomplished much. I must remember this daily. I can give myself credit for what I have done up to the moment when I decide to stop and take it all in. When I can give myself credit for what I have accomplished is when I become motivated and revitalized again. I am responsible for how I encourage myself, and I must. The positive energy I put into myself is building rewards for my body's cells. No, I do not know the outcome of a situation daily, but this is where faith and surrender come in; I must have faith that love is guiding me every day. I must surrender to knowing love is in charge, and I must give over the control of my every day to love. In doing so, I must remember I am love. Therefore, I am relinquishing all control to my deeper self, my soul, who is guiding me in every moment. Sounds strange that I must surrender to myself!

It makes perfect sense that Bach is influential to rap; both are poetry. Then I must ask myself, "How did rap music get a life?"

In my opinion, rap was created through challenging circumstances. A brave soul stepped forth and said, "Listen to me. I'm tired of a certain way of life kicking me down. My soul speaks love fluently, and it has spice. I'm turning it up a notch so everyone can hear my communication, as I don't like to be overlooked."

My soul has truth speaking to me. I must ask it to explain to me what it is I need to hear. Asking for what is desired is not an option, for my mind cannot articulate my soul's highest need. My mind will compromise, but my soul does not. Soul love speaks simply and fluently without impediments of any kind. My mind accompanies my soul, but only in rap music do I know it well.

Megan C Brown

They are two completely different genres of music being played simultaneously. Both need each other, but don't know it yet. Each yearning to be heard felt and nurtured from within, each is playing loudly. Only one is heard at a time. How will my mind and soul share a most sacred refuge?

I think of myself as a ballet performer waiting with my partner behind the curtain. I must listen and be attentive to my ballet partner's direction. I heard my partner say, "Accept your past and forget about what you thought you knew. Please make room for me. I will help you continue writing your soul book. You use toe shoes now. I am trying to teach you how to dance in them. You connect to me while in pain very quickly. As your instructor, I am aware of your listening history. Please listen closer while Bach is playing, I will not speak any louder. Your mind and soul know the music fluently. You trip over your feet because you have not mastered performing in point shoes. Breakdancing is your mastery, but you must master all forms of dance fluently to obtain your doctorate. Keep listening to me, you are almost there. Trust me, I am your soul; I will never hurt you. I must lead you in this dance, but you must know the ballroom, disco, ballet, breakdancing, and the robot. Each will be danced throughout your life's many circumstances. Follow my lead, and I will not let you trip or fall. You are precious to me. I need your feet to dance with me and communicate to more souls with our dance steps. I will be patient with you as you learn your new footsteps wearing your new ballet slippers. You will not fail, I promise. At the end of our performance, roses will be thrown on the stage as displays of endorsement. When you retrieve each rose, you must be careful of the thorns. You do not want to prick your fingers. Each stem was

A Catalyst

created with thorns to protect the exquisite rose sitting on top. Beauty can always be seen. One never has to risk being stuck by holding the stem. When you pull the rose to smell it, notice the veins in the petals. When you hold the rose is when you receive the entire gift this powerful creation is. Without taking the risk, you will have a partial experience. If you want the full experience, you must welcome the possible pain associated with it. If you risk nothing, you will gain nothing new. How will your confidence grow? How will you know what you are missing? You will have declined a course in life's class of faith and promised strength. When you recognize love as being your leader, all fear is removed."

I have been blessed with love, and I do not want to miss it. I want to feel it all with every emotion, every feeling expressed, and every outcome. The dialogue of dance led by my mind and soul with love. Whether my performance is the ballroom, ballet, or jazz, it is a creation in love.

I started with baseball and moved into ballet; I believe both are the same. Each activity requires an individual to go within and find solace and know how to be in the moment. Until I can go within and surrender to whatever the moment is, there can be no unification of love on a grander scale. God and Heaven kept saying, "Acceptance is synonymous with love." Therefore, acceptance and love are the same. I must accept myself and all my life to love myself; there is no separation of self except for the inability to love me.

How can I talk about separation of myself when I am talking about loving myself? If I do not understand I must accept myself, then I am disconnected from my soul. The Second Trinity cannot be had if I do not allow my soul to

Megan C Brown

be who I am and communicate to myself I am love and know I am love in my mind.

The Second Trinity is paramount as I reflect God in living form. It is my belief this must be comprehended by our globe to take away segregation, emancipation, and wars. Mercurial ways of life throughout our world aligned with rules and understanding for love would behoove us tremendously. I am expressing my desire for change based upon what I know to be true from my experience in Heaven. To discuss love as a higher way of being and knowing God and Goddess are the love, I think takes out the separateness of personal belief. Think of living in love definition as a person who desires and supports an establishment of a state, country, and a union of countries around our globe, which in the future will become the state of unification of all people. A state and country are a natural location. What is a natural location is being such from birth? From birth, we are born into love with love while being love. It is my belief then if we do not honor ourselves as being the Second Trinity we are; it is a desecration to God's name.

The science of love keeps on building upon itself if it is understood; what I understand is it-is work, it is much-needed work. As a world, we are so far away from the origin of the self, how did it happen? As both Mozart and Bach pointed out to me in our meeting, greed took over. What is sad about this fact is that humanity has somehow skewed the richness of friendships, family, and happiness, the almighty dollar? Wow! Where is the richness in something that is hoarded, traded, and used to purchase materials? Humanity has mistaken having goods, property, or money in abundance with the richness of having an abundance of some characteristic quality. To each his and her own, but what if the riches of

A Catalyst

love were to become abundant? No one would suffer. It would be impossible. It is not pies in the sky thinking, as my grandfather used to say. It is possible, but it requires us all to work as teammates. This way of being is not a concept, but a reality waiting to be had. As an individual, I must continue to condition myself as the player who makes up the team. I must continue to practice; practice creates skill, the skill being subtle or imaginative ability in inventing, developing, or executing something. To execute from love as the science that it is.

God, Goddess, Jesus, and Archangel Michael told me about the fractionated compound brain theory and three hundred being the daily denominator, but I thought about something else. There is a love potion that exists, I have already stated the ingredients in this book. What if it was put to the test? It would not hurt anyone, but possibly improve everyone. Father Time said to me, "Time does not heal all wounds, only love heals all wounds throughout time."

I believe time is the only component in the growth of a life form like a plant for example. If a life form is nurtured from the beginning with love, I believe it can grow faster, bigger, and not be held back in its ultimate potential despite the restrictions of location. Now imagine if a plant could be directed with love and prove to us all love has no restrictions, what humanity can do with the intelligence quota within a town, city, country, nation, government, and our world. It is exciting to me to know a beautiful difference awaits us all if we just try. We have nothing to lose, but we have everything to gain.

The gentility I am speaking of is my dream admittedly, but I cannot be the only one. There are many other people whom I would imagine feeling outnumbered, but all it takes is practice and word of mouth. My life is different because of what I have experienced in Heaven. As Freddie Mercury sang in one of his songs, 'This could be Heaven for everyone.' He was right.

The magnitude of love also depends on my willingness to forgive. I can let go of all emotions surrounding every incident in my life. In doing so, I can detach from the occurrence and in doing so does not mean it never happened. It simply means I am choosing to redirect my energy to the blooming of freshness that did not exist before I let go of the less-than-love energy I once held. The seeds of love need to be watered, and the soil needs to be nurtured and cared for.

To continue to carry the heaviness of all that I have endured in my life takes a lot of work. To release the original feelings behind memories and transmute them into acceptance seems difficult, but it is possible. The incidents have already occurred and cannot be altered, but the power to alter the course of my energy input is astounding.

Like the bull rider at the professional rodeo who is jostled by choice, I am choosing to relinquish the need to know my outcome. Every ride comes to an end I just don't know how long I will be holding on for in every ride. Sometimes it is best to jump off quickly, but a full ride effect I will determine when I am tired of holding on for dear life. Then when I determine my ride is over, I ask myself if the ride deserved that much attention. Should I have gotten off earlier or later? Earlier is out of the question, but later means I have yet to feel the full effect. What more do I need? I won't know until I get the feeling that I've had enough.

As the rider, I must walk away because I'm done, but I still feel uncertain. Did I give it all I had in me? My

A Catalyst

answer is yes, or I wouldn't have stopped the jostling. What I have realized is as I am walking away, I am also walking into. I am walking into what I don't know, this is where faith comes in. I must continue to have faith that whatever I have walked away from has conditioned me for my next ride. Whenever it is, I will hop on again as the professional rider. I may be a spectator from the stands like with baseball. Hopping on the bull requires every part of me physically and mentally to participate and I must stay in the moment. There is no linear thinking happening. How can I put things in order as I experience them and express them? My thinking process cannot be in a sequential order like a straight line; a straight line from point A to point B would be nice. Nevertheless, as I am being jostled by the other factor it becomes as surrender Archangel Michael spoke of as I am falling over the side of the Grand Canyon. The order is in surrender. Surrender is linear thinking, but the addition is being made to what I feel. What I feel is not completely what is. In surrendering, I am committing to whatever my outcome may be. It is still an orderly fashion from the beginning to the end to accomplish my goal, but with commitment. I am engaged in something that restricts freedom of action from anything else other than the one thing I have surrendered to; I am surrendering to multi-linear knowing that is instinctive committal to self.

How is a multi-linear knowing even possible? Multi-linear knowing is soul alignment with mental alignment and surrender all at once. Why is this necessary? To feel the emotion, energy in motion is soul alignment. To know I can feel what is happening is mental alignment, like point A to point B. To surrender is to commit to the act of energy in motion.

Megan C Brown

Getting back to walking away from the ride when I choose to jump off. I understand that point A began when I got on the bull, and point B was when I chose to jump off. The moment I chose to jump off was when my soul aligned and felt the energy in motion to point B was complete. Surrender is committing to the act of energy in motion in a different direction-when one door closes, another one opens. I am beginning a new point A with the understanding that I don't know where point B is, but my energy in motion will guide me through the mental unknown with my faith and belief in love.

Just like baseball, when I hit my ball, which is the equivalent to my choice I make in my day, I must move forward as far as I am able with all the additional components in place. I must stay focused and be in the moment of each move forward to the outcome, or home base. The big difference is my bases can never be loaded. It is just me as the batter and runner. Just like cricket, you never go backwards in baseball.

Chapter 11
Unification

I am beginning a new soul groove today. I wake up and the song of my energy begins to play the moment I open my eyes. It is happening while I am asleep, but I don't remember; it matters not what I do not remember. What matters is what I am consciously aware of, what energy I put forth, and what I am accountable for. How is it that I am accountable for energy? This energy is a composition of my thoughts, my physical action, conversations with others, and my soul dialogue. It is a complex alignment of different kinds of particles that consist of small amounts of information I create within my mind because every choice is created by my mind.

A composition of myself is like a musical score or a painting. Beat changes and brush strokes. I have mentioned these things before, but of course, there is more. The sounds and colors are like angel wings. Some are soft, fluffy, stiff, iron, gold, or coarse; multitude of varieties depending on the mood of the angel or Archangel. Yes, they have mood changes depending upon love's subjective response to a person or situation

Megan C Brown

being felt. My every day is a painting and a song for our universe. How cool is it that we are each an art form of a sort? Each of us is a display, a masterpiece within the golden thread tapestry that blankets our universe.

If I keep my thoughts in the 528 Hz category or higher like Mozart's music, I will have an easier time in my day. It is not living in denial. Instead, it is living a working test of faith, patience, and strength. What am I trying to say? The love frequency in thought-form is going to be tougher than a chord or note played because I have to consciously think of keeping my thoughts at a higher place above a previous interval of time just before the onset of some other thought. I use my experience in Heaven as the interval of time I choose to think of if my thoughts are less than love-whatever works. Why will I consciously choose to think about happy memories? To bring me up when I am in the bottom of my grooves!

A concerto is the story of my life. They have had a significant influence on me moving forward like the brush strokes keep dipping for the next color, the splash of subtlety, or the bright thick stroke of movement into the already existing organized collection and mixture of various life stories. The experience in Heaven and my every day on earth is coalescing as the braided composition God created for me to bring back and somehow make sense of.

I am enigmatic energy cascading into every moment. I need to nourish love and direct it and feed it with high frequencies like the 528 Hz. My friend asked me if she had to do everything, I shared with her to achieve happiness throughout the world. She admittedly does not want to have to rely on anyone else. I told her all she has to do is accept everyone who is not harming anyone else and encourage them to be accepting of everyone else as well.

A Catalyst

We must be the chain reaction to what everyone in Heaven kept saying to me: "Acceptance is synonymous with love. Acceptance equals love. Acceptance is the same as love. To accept is to love." It's simple.

What more can I tie in with my near-death experience at this juncture? More unification of humanity in a bolder stance to include religions. It was so gratifying to me while sitting in a Catholic mass to hear the speaker ask us parishioners to pray for the Muslims who are about to celebrate Ramadan. It was so different from what I heard as a child in the church. Finally, the Catholic Church began to make more sense to me. Additionally, a Pope seems to be thinking outside of the regular protocol box. As a practicing spiritualist, a person who believes an afterlife is a place where spirits continue to evolve, I am so grateful to Pope Francis for going out on a limb. If I could give him a wish of mine it would go like this: Please, Pope Francis, I ask you to sit with my President, Prime Minister of Israel, President of Iran, King of Saudi Arabia, President of India, President of China, Prime Minister of Japan and come together with a mission for global peace. The Star of David, the Star and the Crescent, and the cross of which Jesus Christ was nailed to are all praying to the same God. Continuing for the good of every Synagogue, Gong, Gurdwara, Mosque, Church to include Judaism, Islamism, Catholicism, Hinduism, Buddhism, Taoism, and Sikhism, I ask you to pray for each in the Vatican. I also wish I could be at the Vatican again, but this time for a mass to include prayers for the above.

What I have seen in Heaven is much more than a unification of the above. I have prayed with the Prophet Muhammad from the Quran. I have prayed with King David from the Torah. I have prayed with Jesus Christ

Megan C Brown

from the Old Testament in the Bible. I have prayed with Charan Singh from the Vedas. I have prayed with Buddha from the Tipitaka. I have prayed with Paramahansa Yogendra from the Bhagavad-Gita. Each is beautiful in its praise to God, Allah, Elohim, Gods, Goddess, Jesus, Prophet Muhammad, and the list goes on. Why will I entail each as having been a part of my structured meetings in Heaven? Because I want the world to know Heaven went against everything, I thought I knew from the Catholic Church. I thank Pope Francis for his quote, "Peace is a precious gift which must be promoted and protected. Never has the use of violence brought peace in its wake. War begets war, violence begets violence."

There is a myriad of ways to be grounded and comforted within the rules of conduct and belief. How we find comfort is by choice. Why don't we pray for everyone to find comfort? There would be nothing lacking for anyone. A fulfillment of self is unscripted as it changes on a moment-to-moment basis. I must feel closely the ground beneath me so to speak and walk through every moment of my life knowing it will bring forth the unknown that will later reveal itself to me. I am a participant, a player if you will, in this life of mine. Whether I am hitting the ball, running the bases, or hitting a home run the proverbial way I am moving forward. The good news is forward meaning growth. Growth means I am not without the flow of energy coursing through me toward the direction of self-myself; a set of qualities that makes me who I am; a degree of excellence settling throughout me, and I accept it. By accepting this statement, I am loving myself.

Always planning keeps the movement and freshness of energy fluid. The fluidity within rigidity I have said before and explained to some degree, but it gets better.

A Catalyst

My energy is a substance that has no fixed shape to the human eye. My substance has no appearance but is a kind of matter with uniform properties. How can this be? I am speaking of the triple compounded love frequency that is perfect in every way, but unforeseen to the human eye because of its frequency speed. What it means to me is freedom and immeasurable beginnings and movement of an unrestrained sort.

My power and right to act, speak, and think as I want without restraint are too extensive to measure. How can this be? Again, it is the triple compounded love frequency that is the scale of balance; a new process of intake and comfort of gradation on a sliding scale of sorts as it slides from moment to moment. I keep sliding into the unforeseen as it creates more frequencies automatically in addition to the ones coursing throughout me. This brings me to the new fraction of life. Oh yeah, there is math throughout every moment. I started thinking about the automatic three-hundred denominator of self. What if the world meant life? When my friend asked if we had to rely on one another to make the positive change happen, my answer was yes. If every soul represented the common denominator of another sort, it would bring us together with no direct human control; self-activating on account of numbers compounded by the triple compounded frequency that has yet to be broken down. God told me I had to write a book and that means it must make sense. Therefore, I am thinking outside of the box God, Goddess, Jesus, and Archangel Michael told me in Synagogue. The zero holds three-billion seeds of love in each, and the three zeros in three thousand represent nine billion souls. That should cover every soul on earth. Create the fraction and keep it fed with unending energy manipulated by love's ingredients adhered to one location. Place the three

Megan C Brown

hundred over the three-thousand and multiply it by two over one hundred. The two will represent both the psychological and physical of every soul. The one hundred is a fractionated compound brain theory composition by God's design. What I am saying is the singular triple compounded love frequency is one-hundred, and the two zeros represent six-billion triple compounded love frequencies inside each of us from the moment of our creation. These frequencies are dormant when I do not use them to love. It does not mean my life will be any worse, but it can be better when I direct my energy like the waterfall with love as my intention.

What freedom means to me is equality for every single soul on the map of our world. It is a generic Akashic record for all that blankets the universes as a five-layer grid. Knowing I must hold myself accountable means I can never turn away from sharing this truth on these pages. The first layer is love. The second layer is compounded denominations of soul fluidity. The third layer is the fractionated compound brain theory. A fourth layer is an objective approach to loves triplicated frequency of a whole component broken up into quad-links. Broken into quad-links by the kaleidoscope effect projecting the ions and electrons throughout the entirety. The kaleidoscope effect is the eighth natural wonder of the universe. The fifth layer and highest elemental component is the fractionated plasma of the universe. Rainbows are a timeless strobe effect breaking up the singular beam creating an apparatus consisting of a tube attached to a set of prisms. A prism of this grade refracts the light's surface that is not angled, but an exactness of gradation composed of several shelves. Seemingly, what composes the temperate elixir is having the particles of a still location with nanoscopic order unveiled as the light

A Catalyst

source under the pressure of the Planck constant. The elixir bank of coagulants is the same one compositing the fifth point representing metal in the Star of David. The second layer fifth point is coagulation of metal in the body and everything that nourishes us. The third layer fifth point is Moses who represents food and metal. The Star of David is needed as the rainbow strobe effect breaks up the singular beam of metals and turns them into gold.

The component of compounds in the love layer is a triplicated scientific theory that is explained throughout the universes by Heaven's standards. A triplicated scientific theory means the grid is cubed. What makes this fourth layer of the graph so intriguing to me is that it is the Star and Crescent. The same Star and Crescent that depicts Islam. Love is the compounded cubed representation of intergalactic love inclusive of every galaxy, moon, star, and planet. As this layer represents every star intergalactically, it expounds the compounded love quotients depicted throughout the entire grid covering every universe, dimension, and plane. This fourth layer is the seventh natural wonder of the universe.

The third star is the sixth natural wonder of the universe. The Holy Trinity is in this layer that acts as the fractionated compound brain theory: the Father, Son, and the Holy Spirit. What is so appropriate in this layer is the number three and the sixth natural wonder. This layer is the composite of music, math, and science. This is the layer that Jesus Christ represents on the cross. Jesus is aligned with God in this layer but is not God. God is a shutter, like a device that opens and closes to expose the film in a camera. His face is on the Shroud of Turin.

Prophet Muhammad is truth in love. The real trinity is God, Jesus, and Prophet Muhammad. They are the unified triple compounded love frequency. They are each a snapshot of history that makes up the composite of the third layer only. They are each what helps make this layer the sixth natural wonder of the universe.

The second layer is the fifth natural wonder of the universe. This compounded denomination of souls is all-inclusive. This is intergalactic soul coverage. The charging station of a different kind. Every soul life throughout is charged automatically by the plasma periscope prism that radiates throughout universes. This way station, a beacon of love, is solar controlled. It is an unending force of suns throughout the entirety of universes charging the white threads connecting to its life source such as myself. A hold that is gentle, but unbreakable. The entire thread is a solidified triple compounded love frequency maximized by inflexible cords of gold. The cords are limitless and in the constant reproduction of self as is the way of the universal love path. The three octaves of the two notes are a continued vibration and subtlety that are triangular notes: a note without end.

There is a continued cloud ring filled with hydrogen, and water vapors that are high up in the sky and undiscovered as of now. It surpasses every planet we know of currently. Additionally, there are clouds throughout this second layer that are not made of water, and clouds that are a mixture of oxygen, nitrogen, and a binary compound occurring as a clear colorless odorless tasteless liquid. This second layer is a phantom probing of earth's equations while replicating the constituents of solar gases surrounding the layers of cloud coverage around every existing planet. This fifth natural wonder is a waterfall of clouds that permeates throughout the second layer of the graphite materials unforeseen

A Catalyst

currently by NASA. What I am writing about in this second layer can be seen by a satellite if programmed with contact lenses of a shadowed sepia hue receptor engine infiltrating black and white photography with a chemical process done on silver-based photographic prints.

The first star and fourth natural wonder are a cascading of the ice formations: a solidified congruent frequency factor based upon rations of elements consisting of every universe; congruent by sizable locations in the force fields that are constantly pulling every element into the hole centered amidst the circumference of a city like clusters throughout the remainder of this layer. What is the ultimate component of unbraided territory throughout the sectors of life formation in the most warming of temperatures to exhibit a wash cycle of sorts for the cleansing of elements? It is a wash cycle existing in idea, but not having a physical or concrete existence. The fluffy feathers of angel wings are intertwined as the buffing post in the hole surrounding the exterior wall of the interior frequencies in physical form as the triple compounded love frequency component actualized in a nearly straight line having the capacity to affect the actions of something.

The triple compounded love frequency component is a breakdown of multiple outside components locked into the fray of consistency in ethereal formations strident of human interjections. The fray suggesting the constant effects of the strain is holography. Holography is a photograph that shows the action of the light spreading across the Akashic record presenting itself in a way that appears three-dimensional. Why will this record fall into the first layer? The first layer is facing up and down but facing up through every part of the layer is what registers

109

Megan C Brown

a beat compound to every soul and ignites the soul with every detail of every outcome. Facing down this record projects a quality governed by the rate of vibrations producing it. It is a monotone pitch unchangeable and unending. Who is the producer? Love is the constant energy never detracting from a solidified substance making up the positive compounds.

A positive compound composition is a free-flowing unit of energy combined with the solution of hydrogen, photons, oxygen, lithium, boron, orbitals, molecules, and deuterium. This stands as a guide to the grid composite solidified throughout the entire space-time continuum. The back and forth of the record are a solid streamline of autonomic systems combing wavelengths into bursts of sound monitored by the idea in the procreation of self. The spectrum of convergence is absolute throughout the entire formation. Withholding the beams of an important compilation to unite under the direction of the center orbital opening in the central nucleus of the eighth natural wonder of the universe coming into fruition of magnitudes of compounded frequencies beating down with a most consistent force to unite the ratio of circumference through the entirety.

It is exciting to me to explain the beams of a literal connection to God uniting under the entirety of all that is. What I am saying is that God, Jesus, and Prophet Muhammad are already united. Judaism, Islamism, and Catholicism are a united golden cord existing right now. The Star of David, the Crescent and the Star, and the cross with Jesus Christ nailed to it are powerful forces. Each is currently unknown as to the amount of love each is producing within the deep cavities of the centralized location excluding nothing. Each only love. All three symbols are in a centralized inactive location in the

A Catalyst

enormous grid. The three religions are one religion. What this means is the photographic shutter speed was inclusive of Prophet Muhammad who was already implanted as the Holy intergalactic image in the third layer of the sixth natural wonder of the universe. Then, many years later, Jesus Christ was born.

The power of the Star of David at one time existed, but when Jesus was preaching from the Torah in homes secretly, He made it more powerful than it had ever been. Jesus was Jewish, but His upbringing was as a non-practicing Jew. It was Constantine and Pontius Pilot who made Jesus a Catholic in the Old Testament Bible they wrote before Constantine murdered Jesus, his wife Mary Magdalene, and Pontius Pilot. There were three swords made that we know as being the crosses each hung from. Jesus Christ's body was removed three nights later by Constantine and moved into the newly built Vatican church in Rome, Italy.

What were three swords are what Christianity knows as being three crosses on the hill. The sword was prominent with the local government called The Knights of the Round Table. Both Constantine and Pontius Pilot were working together. They are not three-hundred years apart as our history books have stated. Jews were forced by The Knights of the Round Table to choose Catholicism or be murdered.

It is difficult to understand the power and ability of love when it has not ruled humanity as we know it. At one time love ruled in the days of Atlantis, but intense desires for power moved at great speed and destroyed the civilization.

The sacred geometry of the galaxies and universes is complex but very refined. A desired state of water takes place throughout the five-layered grid of all that is. The geometrical breakdown of the five-layered grid is beyond a fraction. It is a compartmentalized computation of sorts lingering into the fractionated compound brain theory that can never be answered with an absolute answer. Just like pi, the five-layered grid is approximated and workable. The constant number is 9.37512. For scientists who have used the quotient for holography prisms, it is astounding to have an undecided reasonable outcome as the focus of the universal geometrical equation. Without end, means continued consistency of all that is.

I am going to break down everything I just said in science terminology into layman's terms. I am going to do it in a picturesque explanation using a red rose.

Visualize my red rose as being open with twenty-five petals. Each petal has distinguishing marks, but all are with the same purpose to express the features creating the flower. Let us bring into effect the breakdown of each petal and the overall equation of this one flower. The stem is a constant feed of energy to the rose when unpicked from the soil because of the roots bearing down on the energy field link to the earth's energy core. A structured setting beneath the earth is constantly acquiring new momentum of speed in the intrinsic way only. The body of the rose is situated within the organ of its life on which it acts by using its nerve endings that reach deeply into the earth. They automatically reach down to connect to the life force of this planet that is the central nucleus in the center of the ball that is our planet. The central nervous system that is the control center of the earth is what gives life to everything on this planet. It is a synchronized station subject to this planet only. Every soul born on this planet and every living thing on this planet is orchestrated by the braided unification of love's Divine setting. Kind of like a washing machine setting,

A Catalyst

there is one setting for humanity, animals, plants, and organisms. It is a fractionated geometrical compound conforming with the carbon chain that links with thought patterns from the idea core affiliated with the central universe, or as discussed earlier in the five-layered grid that is the embryonic location of measurement depth penetrating the truth of love in a constant world of energetic diversity.

The impenetrable earth circumference formation of all that is earth holds gently the set of grooves making up the thoughts, events, and emotions encoded in a non-physical plane of existence known as the astral plane, or the Akashic records. This is soul grooving happening at speeds beyond the speed of light. The details and exactness of the universes upon universes are lit up throughout the entire five-layered grid encompassing all space in its entirety. The mathematical variables are numbers and letters with symbols throughout rows of constantly changing frequencies to keep up the triple compounded love frequency in every plane, porthole, dimension, and the universe.

The exploding brilliance of colors is beyond anything obtainable on earth. The explosions of love is a firework display that is a constant throughout the central nervous system of the galactic empirical location in the center of music, science, and math spinning clockwise in geo prism force effects that catapult the opposed force fields of all other stars. The unification of the love barrier is not what a normal barrier is in keeping something out, or from fleeing. Instead, it is an electrical dominance of great importance that magnifies all love quotients to be amplified by the mirrored image of self in an opening of details displayed in a luminescence throughout the body of the intergalactic freeway of love. The openings of

Megan C Brown

deposits accumulated are part of the grooves encasing the frequency spectrum of self. The mind of self-actualizing is a component throughout the intergalactic network engine of all that is. The radiation of love in an uncompromised setting entailing every needed organism in a containment throughout the intergalactic field of dreams scheduled from the dawn of time to inhabit every soul existing. The barometer of love engaged in the mental continuum is not only unbreakable but is unchangeable. The exact purpose of love is to survive. When I think about God, Jesus, and Prophet Muhammad having been woven into the fabric of all that is from the beginning of time I think about the world peace waiting to happen. How can a commitment to change be adhered to if there is no understanding, it cannot?

The symphony of love components is an eternal concern for the well-being of all that is. It plays like a player piano, automatically playing utilizing a rotating perforated roll that is gold. The intergalactic changing of the guard is a classical order of architecture consisting of elements of the ionic order.

Frequently played music accompaniments being played simultaneously one on top of the other is a world order unto itself. The layer over layer is countless and thin holding the exactness of numbers and symbols of what makes up the construction of love patterns in formalities encompassing its position on a scale between two extreme and opposite points. Linear placement is a coming together of two lines constantly vibrating to keep the expansions of endless unification as one in a dual form bringing into effect the monozygotic twinning ratio of self.

There is a thundering effect of cyclical degrees in one constant spot for a forced coming together of electrical

A Catalyst

frequencies in a cylindrical mechanism extending the range of available notes throughout the love path of b triple sharp and c triple sharp. The two notes being played constantly with a mirrored image of itself as an unchanged setting is balancing the needed purpose of identical self-placement. The frequency fixed amount was decided by the combination of the b and c triple sharp unending placement in all that is. The two notes are a discrete quantity of energy proportional in magnitude to the frequency of the radiation each represents.

The radiation units are a matched quantum physics as mentioned earlier. I have properly aligned the mathematical units that are the value of two mathematical expressions equaling one. I have supported the foundation of loves rose with the roots digging in the dirt that is the electrical charge station for the survival of the beautiful flower. The water giving life to this one rose is monumental as it is a direct relationship between two and more measures of loves triplicated compounding throughout the patterning of variances in the geo prism form.

The Heavenly crevices of love are an unyielding golden statue of a treble clef in the center of the waterfall in the center of the universe that includes earth and is a constant cascading of luminescence that is a discrete region of magnetism in ferromagnetic material as a triple compounded love frequency. The light of love ignites this universe and is then amplified by a mirrored effect that is unending throughout universes, dimensions, vortexes, portholes, geo prisms, planes, field formations, and populous of birth cycles throughout every all. This cyclical magnetic beam streams throughout entire vortexes that are encumbered in one location.

Megan C Brown

The field of life is dependent on the abundance of vortexes that are invisible to the eye interwoven throughout spheres making up Heaven's regions. This timeless free universe connection is a length equal to the square root of the standard value cascading over the never-ending trimmings of chards of gold in the central fusion of dynamic pieces constructed as a wall in an outer layer of tissue below the stems and roots of earth growth. The life force is constant at two points in time and space as the linear placement of a solid gold Heavenly carving depicting two souls, white balls of light energy, playing harp in the center of the waterfall that is in the center of the universe. This is perfection.

The earth core is abundant in photosynthesis frequencies that permeate through the thick wall of chakras that are magnetically charged in a straight line up and down in the center. To magnify the seven points, one on top of the other, the fractionated compound brain theory is throughout each ballpoint representing each color chakra. The number one chakra at the top toward the earth's sun in North America is violet. The number two chakra just beneath number one by three inches is white. The number three chakra three inches beneath number two is pink. The number four chakra three feet beneath number three is red. The fifth chakra eight feet beneath the fourth is cobalt blue. The sixth chakra eight feet beneath the fifth is periwinkle blue. The seventh chakra is eight-hundred feet under the sixth and is a rainbow of red rose in color, marigold orange in color, lemon yellow in color, pine green in color, peacock blue in color, and royal purple in color. The symmetry of each chakra point is around the earth's vertical axis. Impending booms of sound are constantly radiating around the chakra central vertical axis. The gloriousness

A Catalyst

of symphonic booms, by timpani, and cymbals, both in b sharp and c sharp are unparalleled in sound fractions three thousand divided by three-million parts per unit of sound. God, Jesus, and Prophet Muhammad are this mathematical equation individually. Make no mistake, these three are united image shuttered photograph in the third layer. United, they are incomparable as the unit of force from a gelatinous goo that is collagen in the photographic process, and simultaneously being a photographic negative image in the print that is stationed as the blanket surrounding the third layer. The unity of this Trinity is unbreakable. They are the triple compounded love frequency as the unified Trinity that is unbreakable.

As the lead original strength of all that is, the Trinity is the momentum and driving force of equality. Let Dr. Martin Luther King, Jr.'s dream be the reality of our world in the twenty-first century.

Chapter 12
Of All There Is to Love

The elements of my life are a piece, by a piece of gold thread woven together as a soul tapestry. My soul is a loving tapestry sewn from conception to the moment I die. Like a magnet, it gleans every moment with full force omitting nothing. Like the Akashic record, it reveals emotions, thoughts, and spoken words. Like a surging wave across the oceans of every emotion, thought, and spoken word around the central column of an inflorescence system rolling into its imaginary, fixed, straight line onshore about which my body rotates around the second cervical vertebra below the atlas and at the top of the atlas, stationed as an alliance of two metaphorical continuums that divide the second cervical vertebra into equal halves. My posture of switching the global axis from left to right hemispheres in the equal halves is a compounded fraction unto itself that is a replica of God, Jesus, and Prophet Muhammad. The excessive amount of love in programming is done at conception with the layered images as blankets of, in order, the Star of David, the Crescent and the Star, God, Jesus, and Prophet Muhammad. This is an order of programming to the finely tuned love frequency I am. Every single soul is exactly what I have just described whether they believe it or not. The governing body of love is unbreakable no matter what the individual soul's belief system is in his or her conscious mind.

It is beautiful to know I was given an order from God while I was experiencing a near-death experience in Heaven. I spent five days in Heaven where I was enrolled in the class after class of love with more than Jesus Christ. He was absolutely a main teacher, but so was Prophet Muhammad, King David, Sitting Bull, Paramahansa Yogendra, Charan Singh, and Quan Yin. Each was devoted to teaching me for the betterment of mankind.

My life has continued to unfold in ways I could never have dreamt of, nor would I want to dream of having. The source of self is miraculous in all ways. I am constructed like everyone else as an intense expression of feelings and ideas with a distinctive rhythm that makes me, me. Praise be to God, Goddess, and all who work in Heaven for their unconditional love. The acumen of philosophy, theology, and religion all wrapped up as one in an incredible way of being are the standards adhered to with an energy that is a binding force for us all. Holding together a strict way of being while being the gentlest of teachers whose precision is an indication of how to behave in every circumstance. Roses and flowers of every kind each was to me. Their sense of humor was surprising and amazing. They represent to me a way of being an uninterrupted chain of an unspoken language that is love. The language that is fluent throughout every one of our beings.

Formerly a giant question mark about what could be existing at the end of my life has been demonstrated by the evidence. Multiple deities cannot be refuted by me.

A Catalyst

Each to me before 2007 was a nice story, but come on; I could not believe there was a man named Moses who parted the Red Sea. Amusement parks were not even created in his period! Why would anyone believe what sounded like another myth? Until I watched that piece of Moses' life review in my near-death experience, I did not believe something like that was possible. Proof? Yes, it was, and there was so much more.

The gentiles never existed until Constantine and Pontius Pilot created the Old Testament Bible, the Vatican church, and Roman Catholicism. Two Jews are the reason for one of the Holy Trinity symbols coming to life on earth, and of course, Jesus Christ himself being nailed to the cross.

God told Noah to build an ark. This miracle was an apparition of God visiting Noah one night as he was praying by himself. God told Noah to find one male and one female of every animal and bird he could find and keep them on the ark until God's next visit to Noah when he would be telling him to prepare for the flood. When it was time to go to safety and ride out the worst storm of over one-hundred years, Moses was also ordered by God to be on the ark with Noah and his family, and all the animals. As the Bible tells it, Noah lived for hundreds of years, but this is false. He was fifty-two when he died of lung failure. Noah grew tobacco and loved to smoke. Moses was sixty-two when he died of natural causes. During Moses' life, he kept journals that are in the Torah. Moses also wrote the book of Job, and some Psalms. Moses was becoming a proselytizer while on the ark with Noah and Noah's family. You see, Moses believed in God and it was he who prayed for Noah to receive a visit from God to tell him his soul purpose. Moses and Noah were brothers.

Megan C Brown

My main reason for sharing what I once considered to be the biggest myths ever created, is to tell God's truth as it was told to me. I have already apologized to God, Goddess, Jesus, Moses, Noah, Prophet Muhammad, and many more for treating these stories as the comic books I once thought they were. Not one of these beautiful souls I am speaking of is angry with me. I cannot think of returning to Heaven without having written this book.

So, for the atheists, agnostics, and religious believers, I can say I believe in all your belief systems. I once lacked the belief in God, I was also a person who believed that nothing was known or could be known of the existence of God, but now I believe, and I know the existence of God.

Heaven's philosophy is diligent, thorough, and extremely attentive to details. Not a thing is overlooked. The perfection of Heaven is miraculous, to say the least. Where else could I have felt more comfortable? I was with an all-consuming way of being and I loved every moment of it. I never questioned whether I would be allowed to come back for more. It was understood from the beginning what was required of me from God's mouth to my ears as He ordered me to write this book. I was inspired by such polite attention and respect given to me. I felt as if each was my friend.

For another way of being to be believed, I am the type who needs proof. I can understand people who think my talking about Heaven is a bit over the top, but I swear I would not believe it myself if I had not been there. It took kidney failure to be my catalyst to an understanding of Biblical, Torah, and the Holy Quran proportions. The Heavenly spheres of science coalescing with love, God, Jesus, and Prophet Muhammad is amazing. The ease with which the creation of the Creator has come to life for me takes all questions out. Mathematics breaks down simply

A Catalyst

the abundance of love for Judaism, Islamism, and Catholicism. Science has created all that is. Science is everything that is living.

My life is unfolding in harmonious ways even though I do not know what will be happening next. I must always have faith and keep looking up even when times get tough. This is much easier said than done I realize, but it is my mantra. I have learned my place in life requires me to fall in line with my process of doing something. Everything is moving forward with my actions playing out. What is everything? Everything is every single piece of my energy helping make up the larger whole linking me to the world and universe. Oh yeah, I am going galactic because it is. Our world is connected to the universe and cosmos any way we look at it. Look up in the sky and see the sun in the day and the stars and moon at night. The creation of delight continues in a multitude of ways. I have characterized my delight with a depth of happiness that is soul felt knowing I am taking part in something so much bigger and better than anything I could have ever dreamt of. I have seen galaxies while I sat at God's table in 2007 when He lifted His hand and opened the dome of Synagogue. This is when God explained everything to me about science, math, and music is the root of consciousness throughout entire galaxies, dimensions, planes, and portholes. Yes, this begins to sound a bit woo-woo I admit, but the truth is what it is.

Because I respect atheists, agnostics, druids, and other peaceful souls who believe in something that falls a bit left or right of center, I must share one of the greatest experiences in Heaven. While I was in my near-death experience, I was taken to a large arena to watch a show that included giant balloon puppets being used as the characters. I do not remember what the show was about, but I remember leaving the arena with Goddess and Archangel Michael. I remember seeing this male figure with black, short spiked-up hair walking in front of me wearing a purple velvet jacket from the Shakespearian period. When he turned around to look at Goddess and Archangel Michael, I remember his face was lizard-like. This was normal in Heaven because it is not just a human stopping ground. Think of the bar scene in the movie Star Wars. That is my description of Heaven in a nutshell, and I love it. The diversity of beings living life on a new planet. Heaven is anti-drugs and alcohol, but you can smoke cigarettes if you want to. If you want to visit a hookah lounge instead, so be it. It is there.

During another visit in my near-death experience, I was greeted by, Prophet Muhammad, Jesus, Archangel Michael, and King David. What a powerful group of males they are! Each sat me down at a small golden table and informed me of Synagogue, the Masjid, and the Catholic Church. This is when I was informed of the five-layer grid. However, one should choose to celebrate Judaism, Islamism, or Catholicism it is allowed. There is the Kotel to pray before with King David as long as you desire, a Masjid led by Prophet Muhammad to pray in as long and as many times as you choose, and a Catholic Church to attend masses led by Jesus Christ as long and as many times as you choose. Archangel Michael is at all locations at one time. Jesus told me he is regarded as the Son of God in Catholicism. He honors Catholicism and gives one mass after another. There is a plethora of love being given in Heaven, and it is magnificent.

For the Buddhists, there is a Temple worship led by Buddha if you choose to pray. There is a Gong for the Taoists led by Quan Yin for as long as you choose to

A Catalyst

worship. The Sikhs worship in a Gurdwara led by Narinder Singh Kapany for as long you choose to. The Native Americans are life scientists in Heaven. Their constant prayer is led by Sitting Bull who encourages each to pray with him if they desire.

The fantastic relationships and cohesive ways of being are a beautiful reality for everyone to have. The constant of putting into effect all points of view so everyone feels at home is remarkable. What would it be like for earth to be cohesive like Heaven? The thought of something like this occurring for humanity is not impossible. It takes dedicated leaders, countries, and states to bring changes into humanity and groups with all characteristics and needs into equal participation. The foundation of love covers everything, but if something is not understood it cannot be obtained. Laws of the universe are such that they are inclusive to everything happening in life whether I believe they exist or not. The beauty of this statement is that no matter what, I can never slow down any vision of love already ingrained in the crevices that are the core of the earth. Visions of happiness, peace, and unification in love's grace are the unchanging recipe and are the umbilical cord connected to every soul existing no matter where the soul is.

Earlier I mentioned the lizard-faced male figure wearing the purple velvet Shakespearian jacket. His soul is as valuable to the universes as mine. I found that experiencing such a combination of qualities walking in front of me to be pleasing to my intellect and moral senses. Knowing the appearance, size, and style of his soul is equally as important to me as I am to him. What an amazing thought!

Evidence for me is knowing what I am saying to be true. It seems so one-sided. I am trying to persuade the world on these pages that all my stories are true; the reality is I cannot convince anyone. What I know for myself is if I am not feeling the truth of something, I will lose interest. How can I better describe in more detail my stories, and why I accept and act following what I have learned as a result of my near-death experience? I must expose more of myself!

Returning to Heaven is something I will do. It is my goal to continue living as if I am always in Heaven. Weird thought, I know, but if I treat people with love, peace, and kindness, my hope is I am spreading a little bit of Heaven in their direction. What better way can I share the happiness I have experienced than to be kind? I don't know of another way.

Venturing off in another direction away from love does not exist. Love is unlimited therefore limitless. How am I going to hide from wide-open intergalactic accordance that sets the stage so to speak for all of life as I know it, and don't know it? I can't. This is what I find to be so intriguing about love. As I have fallen emotionally countless times throughout my life, I had no idea I was being cared for by love. Oh yes, the dance of love is the toughest. As a pupil, I want to ask so many questions, but the dance is never the same. It is constantly changing forward. I think of two moving walkways like the ones at the airport. Except for the dance, the instructor is on top moving in all directions at once, and my moving walkway is directly underneath the instructor's moving forward and trying to keep up with the one on top of me. It is not impossible to keep up, but I must be easily modified to respond to altered circumstances and conditions on a dime. This is not easily done because resistance to change comes into play. This love thing requires great determination and effort on my part, but it

A Catalyst

is so worth it. To be unencumbered in a language of love,
and know it is a soul right from the moment of
conception.

Chapter 13
What Is Our Soul

My love is exactness in being. Like a flower, perfection is unique and nothing else like it exists nor can it for my soul is a one of a kind just like everyone else. Believe it or not, the whimsical wonderment of love can be had the same no matter the distributer. Love is love. The importance of the action and feeling of love is matchless. When you think about feeling love, what else is it? I can't think of anything that will make me feel this good. No man-made material form could ever equate with the primordial life force of all that is.

When I think about the history that is my life, I wonder why I was never encouraged to love because it is a power. Then realistically I say to myself how can instruction be given if it doesn't exist. That takes the responsibility from everyone's shoulders and puts it on to me.

I have mentioned multiple times how powerful love is, and that instructions exist. What I haven't mentioned is how love exists as a buoy to the gateway of the center of the universes. Being on earth links me to stargate number three. This is different from the five-layer grid I have already talked about.

The stargate is a complex structure within a system. A beautiful female named Ezra was introduced to me by Archimedes. She is a star soul who explained this to me as I sat with her and Archangel Michael. The stargate is one of the openings to an existing gateway that prevents the linear spectrum of space from spilling out into the intergalactic space cavities encompassing all that is.

I would like to break down what the system is. It is a microcosm of what forms the necessary base from which love procreates throughout the galaxies. It is a central location track following the main route through the orifice of a standardized generator of sorts. It is a widened gap through the gateway whose main component is a thirty-three and one third gold carat twelve-foot high, by twelve-foot wide, by twelve feet deep fan that constantly blows a twelve-mile per second feed of energy that spreads over all that is by the constant push of recirculating energy of self in the mouth of the deepest depth of space.

The stargate itself is a myelinated tissue in the central love system that is the housing station to the intergalactic intersection, a point at which lines and pathways intersect and branch out from the central connecting point. The stargate's purpose is to come together and form one mass, or whole, to bring love energy together as a blanket uniformly distributed as the tough yet elastic invisible fabric. How is the stargate cared for? There are gnomes, like the ones I saw watering the garden around God's house in Heaven, who are stationed inside of a star platform. The star platform is a thirty-three and one-third carat gold building with special machinery

A Catalyst

inside connecting itself to the orbiting suns in every location throughout every galaxy. The building is a grid of its kind. The thirty-three and one-third carat golden building is an actual pattern of electron density forming in an atom by one or more electrons that represent a wave function. The wave function is a spray of zillions of triple compounded love frequencies that are the constant washing of energy repeated endlessly.

There are three-hundred gnomes in total and they are not gold. They are like the human body make-ups, but only their souls keep their bodies animated. They are approximately fourteen inches high and expel the largest quantities of love rapidly and forcefully.

There are three-hundred suns in total throughout every galaxy, dimension, plane, and star graph. They are charged not only with vitamin D, but also with a love's ratio that is incalculable as the heat measure forces mass production in the sun itself as the system for detecting the presence by sending out pulses of high-frequency electromagnetic waves that are reflected off the sun, back to the thirty-three and one third carat gold building that is the star platform.

There are three-thousand moons in total throughout three of the galaxies, all twelve dimensions in each of the galaxies, all twelve planes in each of the galaxies, and all three-star graphs in each of the galaxies. The starfield support for these moons is located on an axis at the bottom of the vertebrae that is the chain link from the top of the starfield, to the bottom of the starfield. They are vertical in the linear measurement of magnifying power. Every moon is charged with vitamin D and a love ratio that is also immeasurable due to the constant reproduction of heat measure forcing mass production in the moon itself as the system for detecting the presence by sending out pulses of high-frequency electromagnetic waves that are reflected off the moon, back to the thirty-three and one third carat gold building that is the star platform for the suns as well.

The gateway of the center of the universes has the makeup of a celestial force in one opening that is a fan blowing the same amount of love in Heaven throughout every all. The spreading ratio is a build-up of twelve miles per second pushing right behind twelve miles per second, and so on infinitely. This is a never-ending love push.

The growth of love is constant and a natural course of action taking place no matter what. The outflow of love is a task that has been happening since the dawn of time. Remembering it is the most powerful energy that exists explains why our planet and others are still in alignment in the universes.

When push comes to shove, it is always loves alignment happening intergalactically. Why is love such an important topic of conversation to me? Because the quantity of love never varies in value. Having made this statement again I reflect on my life and have to ask myself if I want to put my energy toward love, or do I want to keep drudging up a history that makes no change for the better in my life? The answer is always going to be love. Love owns my mind, body, and soul. I am saying I belong to and am related to love based upon the history of soul factories.

What is a soul factory? A soul factory is an achievement of energy in a light form specifically created for the body that carries it. A soul creation is unparalleled in all the creations. It is the specific animator for the body, the animal, the reptile, the bird, the bugs, the invertebrates, and the ocean. The soul is our internal fire. Its heat measure is the equivalent of an individual sun

A Catalyst

and an individual moon. It is miraculous the source of energy that is within each one of us.

It took my near-death experience to introduce me to myself. It feels weird to write it like this, but it is true. One of my soul purposes is being a mom. My other soul purpose is to write this book God told me to write. What was my soul purpose before I was a mom? I believe it was working and taking care of myself. I admit taking care of myself now after my near-death experience has different avenues. I must now take care of my spiritual self because I did not use to. I meditate every day and practice staying in the moment. I eat properly, I get enough rest, I exercise, and I write. Most important is I accept myself for who I am. I believe accepting myself is another soul purpose.

How is accepting myself part of my soul purpose? While I was in Heaven, God and the rest kept telling me acceptance is synonymous with love. What I have come to realize is I am accepting my soul stories. Every moment that is woven throughout my soul book-the eternal keeper of all my histories. I do not remember all my histories, but I help myself along by telling myself I accept even the stories I don't remember. I must because they are all a part of me and who I am. I may not consciously remember most of the stories from multiple incarnations, but my body remembers. The cell memory is still in full swing.

My story of now is what I must work with as it is the rawest. There is not only one story to look at, but many beginning back to my childhood. How to balance those stories with now or close the chapters of then and focus on the chapter of now. I have chosen the chapter of now. What I have done is recognized the story of now is current and most important, but the stories of then are collaborative insights into who I am and why I am the

133

way I am. Yet the old stories do not define me. They rather place me in a constant position of control of myself. Will I choose to react to situations from a historical place in my life that is only partial and outdated? Or will I choose to react to the situations from a fulfilling place within that is entirely knowledgeable and comfortable in the position of now? It is up to me.

My love for myself is what I need to do throughout all that transpires in my life. It is a vast continuum of feelings and thoughts, but all pointing to the one source that is love, my soul. My soul chambers are concise and the thread to eternity.

The interior of a soul is comprised of five chambers. A complete composition of each chamber generates soul alignment. Alignment is a moral perspective of thought that helps make up a straight line of chakra points from top to bottom. A chakra is an invisible point being a non-physical energy point located in every human body. There are seven chakras in total. Number one is in the center of the top of the head. Number two is the throat. Number three is one's soul or heart chakra. Number four is the belly button. Number five is the reproductive organ or base chakra. Number six is each femur. And number seven is the top center of each foot between the toes and the ankle.

The number one chamber is dialogue. The number two, the chamber is feeling. The number three, the chamber is communication. The number four, the chamber is music. The number five, the chamber is science. The first three chambers are each composed of three veins. Number four is one vein. Number five is one vein. Patience is blanketed around every individual soul.

Dialogue is the first chamber in vain number one and is how we articulate with life. The second vein is how

A Catalyst

an individual soul speaks with the mind. The third vein is a mind and soul alignment, articulating as one with, a unified, mind/soul fluency, eternally.

Feeling in the second chamber is eternal. In vain number one is how our mind articulates with experience, throughout our soul being. The second vein is how our soul reacts and responds to the mind. The third vein is how the mind answers with the soul.

Communication is eternal. In vain number one is how our mind speaks with our soul. The second vein is how our soul speaks with our mind. The third vein is how our soul answers our mind.

Music in the fourth chamber is the mind/soul eternal composition. Science in the fifth chamber is the fluent mind/soul eternal dance.

Every life has multiple memories, connected to every experience in every life, affecting the soul. Incarnations will be a struggle if all three veins in dialogue, feeling, and communication have not been satisfied in achieving each goal, making up the composite of every individual's lives to this now. What has not been dealt with at the end of a life your soul just departed, will automatically become a lead role in your next incarnation. One's mind and soul have a duty to complete all unfulfilled obligations in each contract commitment we signed before incarnating.

One's reason must continue to be honoring every feeling one connects with. Feelings are connected to our entire being. Our soul's memory constitutes the exactness of each event. Everything learned before incarnating is erased at birth.

Science has proven exercise strengthens an area of the body being used in repetition just like the energy of prayer used as a repetition in the mind. Prayer energy is invisible in thought but can make a difference when used in repetition in any circumstance.

Laws of math and science have proven a positive connection to a positive create another positive. The positive for this example is thought. Exercised positive energy results in positive change. When positive energy dominates continually it eventually eradicates all existing negatives. A prayer is an act I choose to participate in within our universe for a positive outcome.

Chapter 14
Of All There Is to Love

The petals on a rose are marked as the fingerprint of another kind. Every petal has a purpose on the one rose. Each is a blanket created to cover the filament, anther, stigma, style, ovary, and hip. The delicacy is impossible to understand. How can the strength of such daintiness ever exist to protect such beauty? As the four walls of a home surrounding me, the petals of a rose are to its occupants.

Why is there such division outside of Heaven? Why can't the way it is in Heaven just be transposed to earth? It can be, but like a muscle, the ways in Heaven must be used on earth.

When in a way of being that is Heavenly, I must always treat another person as the rose they represent. The make-up of the human body is as miraculous as the flower. Think about the mind, the ability to feel, our organs inside of our bodies, and our nerve endings. I will respect each person as the same type of daintiness each is. We are all a living miracle.

Megan C Brown

If I were to step back and refocus each situation I encounter as being a targeted agenda for love, imagine the healing that could occur. A worldwide occurrence of healing is waiting to be had. What makes my dialogue based upon my near-death experience the way? I don't know about anyone else's way. Why not start somewhere where a course is splayed out to follow? There is nothing to lose.

Imagine a firework display with an explosion and the colors that eventually happen after the fuse is lit. I tell my story as an offering to help a world fuse to be lit. An explosion of love with multiple colors is a fabulous thought during my day. A world of healing amid crisis and dismay can occur, but we must help one another get there.

My fantastic ride on love's energy has helped me ground myself emotionally. It is not easy, but it is achievable. I have spoken of the wave surge, and it is. A surge can surge in one day. I think it all depends on how I mentally dislodge myself from connecting to what could be dark crevices of my history.

When I say dislodge, I am removing from a position of power and authority what my mind will hold on to. I want to break free of what could way me down emotionally so I must keep my mind on a clear course to fruition of love. It seems so difficult at times to disconnect, but it's all about disconnecting and reconnecting to what I want to feel. Do I want to feel sad, or do I want to feel in charge?

I am honored to be a part of the most incredible gift every soul is given. I am a participant with a galactic concourse that is ever-changing to accommodate the influx of infinite positions of love.

A Catalyst

I have a responsibility to act and react with aplomb throughout my entire life. It doesn't matter the situation at hand at any moment, what matters is how my energy is used around it.

Why will I continue to act following what I can't see or receive a confirmation on in any one of my days? Because I have seen enough to understand what I am saying is true and taken very seriously throughout every galaxy.

Archangel Michael told me to let everyone know that Psalm 91 is powerful. The moment this prayer is begun, He is infusing your soul with the psalm. He also wants the world to know being a Christian is not necessary to receive the protection you ask for with this prayer.

Prophet Muhammad would like me to share with everyone the following prayer. "In the name of "The God," the infinitely Compassionate and Merciful Praise be to "The God," Lord of all the worlds The Compassionate, the Merciful. Ruler on the Day of Reckoning You alone do we worship, and You alone do we ask for help Guide us on the straight path. The path of those who have received your grace not the path of those who have brought down wrath, not of those who wander astray Amen." Anyone can say this prayer and be received with grace. It is not necessary to be a part of Islam to receive the ceremonial peace from this prayer. Prophet Muhammad wants humanity to remember love divides no one. Born from different mothers, skins of all colors come together as brothers. That's the beauty of Islam!

I believe it is our job as a soul, whether we are atheist, agnostic, Jewish, Catholic, Muslim, born again Christian, Buddhist, Taoist, Sikh, or any form of honoring the life, we are obligated to be a participant in repairing our world.

It was during a meeting when it was revealed to me the basic requirements of life. It was so simple when it was explained by God that love is needed for everyone. Love is the driving force in every religion that does no harm. It is the tool that was shed for me in Catholicism that strengthened my path to God. Now I understand the tool as being the branches on the tree that is rooted in the ground of Catholicism within me. This religion anchors the brotherhood of love through Christ as being our catalyst. Truly Catholicism became more to me than a mass to attend, prayers to recite, and the body and blood of Christ to eat and drink at the mass. The once mystifying experience of church is now a cultivated understanding of communal laws to keep me as an individual aligned with the order to achieve Heaven. Without the order would be a complete lack of understanding on how to achieve the kind of comfort my soul wants.

During my visit, Archangel Michael began to explain comfort to me in a most incredible way. He told me my soul and everyone else's soul needs a soul pattern. A soul pattern is when our actions give regular form to the energy that is action played out in the individual history book that is our Akashic record, or the keeper of everything. My soul pattern relies upon the mass of the mind. The mass of the mind is a large body of matter having no definite shape. In this body of matter, a world of living takes place. Life of the mind is so complex, its distributors have yet to be discovered in the gray matter.

The gray matter is currently an area of unknown subjects comprising a course of study all by itself. This is fascinating to me because there is so much more to be done to help humanity in countless ways. According to

A Catalyst

God, when the gray matter is spoken to as a specific student, it helps retrain the rest of the brain. Record information and play it back speaking to the gray matter area as if it is a specific student enrolled in a course of understanding. The repetition is what changes the fractionated compound brain theory. In other words, the numerator can be set as a certain number with communication to this area of the brain at any given moment. This is an opportunity to manipulate with love the daily principle or standard by which something may be decided. Why not let the quantitative relation between two amounts showing the number of times one value is contained within another be the deciding factor?

Music is a soul pattern unto itself using various rate vibrations constituting a wave in an electromagnetic field, as in radio waves and light, measured in seconds. The music repetition of rhythm and beat is orchestrating a scientific boom plateau in an area around the ring of command that is the brain stem. The brain stem is a transfer of extreme force with endurance to withstand every event no matter what the situation. Every lifetime is seeded in the brain stem and the soul.

A small area called the medulla oblongata is a major structure of the brain stem located in the lower half. It is responsible for the regulation of the heart rate, breathing, blood pressure, digestion as well as controlling several involuntary functions such as vomiting, sneezing, and coughing. This part of the brain gives messages to the spinal cord that is connected to the body. The medulla oblongata contains both myelinated and unmyelinated nerve fibers, called white matter and gray matter.

The spinal cord is comprised of neural pathways. Messages travel from the brain to the body having the quality and ability to be passed from neuron to neuron

141

through junctions called synapses. This process continues until the message reaches its destination, such as muscles, glands, or other non-neural cells.

Referring to the gray matter and the medulla oblongata, each is working simultaneously for the body. If doctors or scientists were to program the gray matter with positive actions and processes as being emotional support and encouragement, the body itself could be healed of any irregularity on a cellular level. Cells are the basic structural and functional units of the human body and there are many different types of cells. The tissues and organ cells themselves perform specific functions in the human body including the epithelial, muscle, nervous, and connective tissues. An organ consists of two or more tissues that perform a function such as the heart and stomach. God told me the brain tissue is a linear format from the head to the feet. The brain speaks every language of the body. To incorporate a manipulative agenda of healing with the gray matter by voice, touch, and or music would begin a worldwide unification of healing on multiple levels.

Our brains are the gateway to a source of healing that would bring humanity one step closer to soul development. An advancement of this caliber would be fantastic. The expansion of concern about and well-informed interest in this type of development would produce an abundance of understanding that would, in turn, create peace, would then cause unity, and finally equate to love.

Chapter 15
What Else Happened in Heaven?

During my near-death experience with God and Goddess, I was taken to Their home. What I saw was a modest home with bright colored flowers surrounding it. Before we entered Their home, they took me down a path in front of the house that went into what looked like, from the outside, as being a rock waterfall. This was an outdoor room underneath Their home with a pool inside to swim in, and a waterfall that looked straight out across Heaven. I asked Them if I could swim in my clothes in the pool for a few minutes because it was so beautiful. They told me I could. I was so excited I swam right over to the edge looking out to a most beautiful view. I remember the colors of the scenery being like a Maxfield Parrish painting. I saw birds flying in the sky, I saw beautiful trees, I saw a lake, and I felt completely at peace. God and Goddess were sitting in the golden chairs on the lower surface of the room above the pool stairs watching me. All of us were quiet until I heard God ask me to get out of the pool so I may follow Them inside Their house. I walked up the stairs and stood before Them. Angels flew in and changed my toga so I would be dry for the rest of my visit.

Megan C Brown

I followed God and Goddess out of the room back on the path up to Their home.

I remember God opening the sliding glass door and Goddess walking in first, then me, and then God. I looked at the unassuming living room and saw Jesus sitting on one of the couches with His wife Mary seated next to Him. Jesus pointed at the couch across from Them and asked me to be seated on it. I followed His orders and Goddess sat to my left on the couch. God was seated in what reminded me of being a recliner between the ends of the two couches across from the fireplace. I remember seeing what looked like family pictures on the living room table and the mantle above the fireplace of all of Them. The kitchen was off the living room behind God with golden Angels cooking in it. I also remember seeing the beginning of what looked like a hallway, and to the right of it was what I would call a study. There were books on the shelves in bookcases that looked old in appearance.

Jesus began signaling with His hand to come in. I looked behind me and Archangel Michael and Prophet Muhammad were standing at the glass door. Archangel Michael slid it open, and both entered to stand between Jesus and Mary's couch and the fireplace. They smiled at me, and God began to speak. "I have ordered you, Megan, to be here with Us for an important reason. We are aware of your dedication to the pages coming to life. I have orders from Holy Spirit to tell you more. Please make yourself comfortable as We explain a few more things to you."

Jesus picked up, "We will be with you every day. My goal in this now is to explain love in a global way for the simplest understanding to occur separately from the scientific breakdown. It is as it should be the division in

A Catalyst

the world as a choice has dictated the outcome without concern for others. The choices to ignore mounting cries for help are unacceptable. We want the world to know We are a union here in Heaven for the good of all. We have been written in the fabric of all that is as permanent. The sheet We are covers every universe and galaxy applying Us as the foundation of love from the beginning of time. The three of Us are the imprint in the construct and arrangement of spirituality. We are throughout the parts and elements of the branch of science that is the structure and internal workings of space. Archangel Michael is the Star of David."

Prophet Muhammad began, "I am Islam. Therefore, Islam is an imprint throughout the parts and elements of the branch of science that is the structure and internal workings of space. I am covering the galaxies with love just as God and Jesus are."

Archangel Michael started, "I am Judaism and the Prince of Israel. Please let this be known. Israel is cared for and protected by Me."

Goddess commenced, "Prophet Muhammad and I are the exact models of the Middle East. We are and have been praying the Quran for the entire earth world. God is the Creator of all that is. We are the prayers for all that is created."

Jesus began, "I too am a prayer of the Old Testament and the Torah. I pray both books because I must. I am a believer in both. It was God and Archangel Michael who presented Themselves in apparition form to King David. I know because I was there as well."

As I sat on the couch, I noticed each was looking at me with a pleasant smile on Their faces. I couldn't help but wonder again how I could be so lucky to receive this information to write about for this book. I had to ask,

Megan C Brown

"God, Goddess, Jesus, Mary, Prophet Muhammad, and Archangel Michael, please help me understand how I can write this beautiful information like a person with no affiliation to a Synagogue or a Mosque. I want to be believed with my truth. I want everyone to know the beauty of how You work in unison as I know it to be true."

God's thoroughness began, "I have been given orders from Holy Spirit whose executive power supersedes My own. You are a devoted soul to love and We all know it. You will continue to write the information We give you and not worry about how the information will be distributed. We have that figured out. We will guide you every step of the way and place on your life path those who will participate in bringing forth all of this information."

I humbly replied, "Blessings received God. I want to please all of You. I am a bit more nervous hearing about how Holy Spirit is involved. When I think about going to church, it is a requirement the congregation always pray to Holy Spirit. Now I am sitting before all of You. With everything that has been shared with me so far, God, Jesus, and Prophet Muhammad, You are the Holy Spirit. I mean this is what I understand right now. Do I understand correctly?"

God continued, "You are a student who is paying attention. Yes, we are Holy Spirit. We are the three interwoven throughout all of space and time. We are uniting for you now as We did at My table in Synagogue. We love you, Megan. We want you to tell everyone Our love is limitless and unconditional. We are a part of the creation of every soul no matter what. It is raising the consciousness of humanity We wish to do to progress everyone to a higher mental state. It will be done. The judgment of one another will eventually be a thing of the

146

A Catalyst

past. Unification will be the way of being one will want to represent."

Goddess began, "We have absolute faith in you, Megan. We are with you at every moment and hear your every thought. You are a child of Ours. Please be gentle with yourself as you are a beautiful person and the creation of God. God makes no mistakes."

Archangel Michael continued gently, "It takes courage to step out from the masses. I know what I speak of. I am a crowd of one. I do not need to explain myself when I choose to serve love. I force love to prevail against all evil. It is God's will I be in love in My mind to know it completely. I think only love. Therefore, I only love. Everybody who chooses to think about love is assisting the energy in branching out throughout the universes. This is the law of the universe."

Prophet Muhammad began, "The laws of the universe are a recipe of love construction. My eternal love is a triple compounded love frequency triplicated by the universal fraction of love that is God, Myself and Jesus. Three-hundred divided by three-hundred divided by three hundred is the quotient, the degree and amount of the quality and characteristic of loves superior force in all that is. My quotient of self is built with that of God and Jesus. I am one force of the Holy Trinity. We look to one another for the good of all. When We met you at the golden table after your life review, we knew there was much more information to give you."

Jesus began, "I am the truth of love in every direction. This means simply from the foundation of being created during conception, I am your love frequency in your mind. Prophet Muhammad is your love frequency throughout your body. God is your love frequency throughout your soul. We are each linked on a cellular level throughout every human, animal, bird, fish, crustacean, and rock, compounded by the galactic force of every that is space. Our love vibrations are automatically intertwined by all energy outlets that are connecting Us by loves movement that is a constant beam fraction to every soul throughout the entirety of all existing space."

God stated, "I am the most powerful conduit to all souls as the triad force I am. You know Jesus as being the Son of God, Prophet Muhammad is, too. I am alerting the world through this book of the exact ancestry to bring together a whole awareness. May forgiveness be victorious and successful in every part of humanity. Only when acceptance becomes aligned with your thoughts will new soul patterns be created. Your mind thoughts are communicating always in all ways to your soul. Your mind thoughts are a regular and intelligible form used with repetition to shape your soul design. The soul design is a constantly changing sequence of elements built upon emotional responses to life. It is the Akashic record of every thought, spoken word, and feeling. Each is coalescing as the intrinsic map layered as the complete work of loves artistry unique to every individual soul."

Goddess began, "My role is not understood as of this now. I love the range with which every soul produces by way of the rhythm that is the mind, body, and soul connection. The individual rhythmic soul vibration of love in the Holy Trinity is Me. I am a constant movement around the axis of the system of loves golden fan that is connected to every soul creation. My endless substance is eternally spilling over the fountain within the center of every soul making up every creation. I am your internal flow of love that is the Holy Trinity."

A Catalyst

Archangel Michael continued, "The Star of David is who I am. The Star and Crescent are who Prophet Muhammad is. We are blanketing every soul creation. We love one another and work as one force united by the mind-muscle that belongs naturally to every creation. Everybody is the Star and the Crescent. Every soul is God's love injection moved by Goddess' rhythmic cyclical action."

Chapter 16
Who Am I Now as A Result of Heaven?

When I think about who I am as a result of all I have met in Heaven, I am still amazed at Their faith in me. I feel honored at the extent to which Heaven has happened in my life. Heaven has opened my eyes to the many avenues of love expressed honestly by way of the arts, religion, spirituality, and other manifestations of human intellectual achievement regarded collectively. As I sat with Paramahansa Yogananda reading through Sanskrit, or while I sat with Prophet Muhammad reading through the Quran, I was engaged with the knowledge of religions that were created by way of peaceful warriors for God. Each one collectively brought to life a format by which belief of a higher consciousness exists and is directly connected to God Himself.

One of my favorite memories when Jesus, Prophet Muhammad, Archangel Michael, and I sat next to a lake. We were casually sitting on the ground discussing the different theologies. I asked each question and was able to hear the ease with which each explained and described the evolution of cultural governing bodies was intoxicating. Each breath of love was a gift to me as I sat listening to a history of another kind situated around me.

The most impressive formula for peace exists in Heaven. With all the diversity among religious beliefs, this peaceful way of being is woven throughout the detailed coordination of a complex operation involving many souls. Each soul holds an attitude based upon choice but overall is aligned with a way of being by way of the congruent setting of the Holy Trinity Infinitum. If everyone would set aside one day a week as 'Heaven Day,' like earth day on April 22nd, and focus only on eradicating judgment for one another, all I can say is, wow! The one day a week becomes four times a month and so on. The energy of each of the days would transport a new focus and be fueled with compassion toward a specific agenda. An agenda to love one another by way of acceptance of one another. It can be implemented like a national monument. Nationally we must count on brave souls who can step outside of the pack and stand up for equality without the worry of ramifications. Consequences of a harmonious action or event of this level could not only be inspirational but an instrument to furthering unity in our current worldwide deficit of acceptance. Let us reach out to one another and say blessings received for your earth contribution of acceptance.

My days of previous dismay are flowers of another kind. Each is a fingerprint on my soul filled with references to loves fierceness. Instead of love's gentleness being felt with warmth, I have felt the cool temperatures set in and stay for a while. I had to work toward healing the condition of discomfort. It takes patience, but patience

A Catalyst

is a requirement no matter what. Literally a capacity to accept or tolerate delay, trouble, or suffering without getting angry or upset. Courage and determination for my ultimate outcomes are necessary as well. What I do not know is what becomes the actual gift from dismay.

Someday I might ask myself if what has happened to me in my near-death experience in Heaven is still fluid throughout my lifestyle. My answer will always be yes. The experience was intense and filled with thinking about ways of being I never would have thought of on my own. It was distinct. It broke the foundation of what I once thought about as being normal. What broke away was like shedding. The new foundation was already in place and already holding me up. The absolute formula of who I am and who I was during that moment of leaving my body has not changed. I am still connected to God, Jesus, Prophet Muhammad, and Heaven.

What it means to me to accept God as unequivocal is safety. I know I am protected by the greatest force of love. I have experienced the different elements of love joining as a team. What was once different to me is now felt as being the same. I witnessed cultural differences, religious differences, and gender differences. A soul is not a culture, gender, or religion. It is a white flame burning in our bodies.

While sitting in church, I began to reflect on how I once felt going to a place of worship. Over time I began to have strong feelings about why the church was behaving in a way that suggested it had higher standards or more noble beliefs than was the case. I did not hear the unity of our world being spoken about, so I dropped out in my early twenties. What I began to do was be a hypocrite. I thought my reasons for not showing honor to God, Jesus, and Heaven in the church were the way they should be.

Megan C Brown

Somehow, I thought I was being inclusive of the rest of the world by steering clear of Catholicism. I had it all wrong, but I'm jumping ahead.

It started to bother me when I heard at every mass I attended in the Roman Catholic Church profess it was the only way to Heaven. I wondered how a religion could be so sure of itself. It was not doing it for me any longer, but I didn't fall back on any other religion. Where was I to turn? I did not turn anywhere, not even into myself, I had no idea I could. I continued aimlessly moving forward in my life, but I had no solid belief or understanding of what reality was. This is a heavy statement to make. What was the state of things as they existed, as opposed to an idealistic idea of life? Where did life begin? I had no idea. What I didn't know was that I was not alone.

I was unaware of what I was moving forward to, but it didn't matter. I did not know I had a purpose. What could my purpose have been in a world filled with wars, media-driven powers, and in my opinion no collective reason to be friendly with one another? How or why would I come to such an understanding? Because nothing of the contrary was being taught, nor did it exist in my life.

As someone who began to live lacking belief in the existence of God, while at the same time believed that nothing was known or could be known of the existence of God, I now stand corrected. I have been shown the light, God, Jesus, and Heaven.

It had to be kidney failure, an experience so painful I was going to be forced into a position to be the student and listen. There was no walking out of this life class. It took me thirty-eight years to begin to be whom I was born to be. It is a long time, but it takes what it takes. My

A Catalyst

purpose-driven life was realized when everything I loved was going to possibly be gone.

What I have come to appreciate is the acceptance of the old beliefs I could never have done myself. The labor of love that was chipping away quickly during my five days in Heaven has opened me up to a wider understanding that is the world I live in.

Where is a person supposed to begin telling a story like this and categorize it according to importance? It is puzzling. Everything is important and of great value to me because of an event that began as unwelcomed but has been felt throughout my entire being as the greatest gift and awakening I could ever have had.

Chapter 17
Get Ready

I have been to the light, walked through the clouds, and been greeted by Jesus. Where Jesus to me was once a fairytale character, I now revere Him as the peaceful warrior He was and still is. Jesus introduced me to Archangel Michael whom I had heard of growing up in the Roman Catholic Church as being the destroyer of evil. I have no doubt any longer the beautiful Archangel exists. I revere Him as well for being the warrior I heard about in church. Then, while I was sitting at God's table in Synagogue, I was introduced to Prophet Muhammad, a Muslim name I had only heard of and lacked knowledge of His peaceful ways as the Prophet He was and still is for the Middle East. I met God Himself after I was led into Synagogue by Jesus, Mary, Archangel Michael, El Morya, and St. Germain. It was astounding, to say the least. He exists and I am living to tell about Him.

I grew up saying a prayer called 'The Profession of Faith.' One line refers to someone "seated at the right hand of God the Father almighty." This is Jesus being talked about, and it is true. Jesus is seated to the right of God. I was seated to Jesus' right, and I saw giant wings on multiple Archangels seated to my right filling this side of the table, down to Melchizedek who sat to the left of Goddess who was seated straight across from God.

What could I say when Gaius Julius Caesar came in to stand between Jesus and me to announce His truth for the world? Well, I could only promise Him I would put His truth in this book, and I have. The unbelievable powers I had only read about I had now been surrounded by in a most amazing meeting.

I cannot say enough about Prophet Muhammad. This beautiful soul who was the Prophet for the Middle East has many truths to be made known as well. Most importantly how He is assisting the entire world with love. His precious ways are misunderstood by those who are not Islamic.

Archangel Michael and the multiple Archangels I saw to my right were beautiful with giant feathered wings, golden wings, and iron wings. It was amazing to think each existed and was all seated to the right of God. I saw golden cherub Angels that never said a word as they fluttered around God's golden table in Synagogue and throughout some of my experiences in Heaven. They are involved with specific patterns of another kind. Angels and Archangels are assisting our world with the healing of our souls. All we must do is call on Them, and They are by our side assisting us because They know each of us has free will and choice, so they must abide by God's rule to be invited by us to help us. There are exceptions when Angels and Archangels step in to help by God's instruction.

My encounter with the perfection of this level was astounding in every way. How could it not be? One minute I did not believe in anything, and the next I was being greeted by God's son Jesus. What I have come away

A Catalyst

with is much, but most importantly the lessoned desire to judge others. I have learned everyone is judged the moment you begin to watch your life review. Why judge one another with such intent and rationalize the judgment with a false mental comfort of power and influence over others? It does nothing for our individual highest good.

My surprising, impressive experience has had a lasting impression on me because it was a soul event that took place. Admittedly, if I had not experienced this I would still be questioning if God and Heaven exist.

Seeing as how I am a true believer now; I desire to advocate for God and Heaven. Having made this statement, I am also respectful of those who do not believe in either because of my experience. On the following pages, I have splayed out a multitude of actualities based upon meetings I had.

While I was faced with death from an extremely rare autoimmune disease called TTP-HUS, I was faced with life at the same time. I mentioned the life review, but I was also witnessing a way of life that is Heaven. Heaven is a religious mecca and a religious gathering place for all the love. It is a theologian's dream.

When I was experiencing my near-death experience, nothing seemed to make more sense to me. It was the most all-inclusive establishment I have ever attended. I had a sense of great respect in my just being myself, and I witnessed this in every interaction I had. Everyone I interacted with was a straight shooter of love for God.

Everything about me was changed from the inside. To have changed from my once internal place of comfort was as if I had gone into Heaven as a caterpillar and exited a butterfly with beautiful colors. Every time I think about what it was like to have been to this place I once thought of as a myth, an idea, and a belief, I quickly recollect the fun and joy I experienced while I was there.

I hope to share on the following pages my truth and help spread excitement about what is to come when God takes us out of our life. The end of our lives is not something to fear. Instead, it is something we can feel a deep admiration for from my observation, facts, and events. How can I feel comfortable making a definite expression of something in my writing based upon what some may say as being nothing more than a drug-induced experience? I never had a doctor shut down my brain function. I had doctors trying to keep me alive and keep my other organs from stopping, kidney failure, blood clots, and my blood platelets dropping from the TTP-HUS. Yes, there were a few things my body was faced with during the critical evaluation, but there was never a need to shut down any part of my body. As one nurse said to me, "We thought you were dying and we're trying to help you get comfortable."

Just when I thought my life was coming to an end, I learned it was only just beginning. It is this beginning I speak of I am imparting on the following pages.

Chapter 18
Heaven is for Real

To have been in the presence of what I now consider to be eternal greatness deserves more of an explanation.

My atheist self was greeted by Jesus Christ; a leader for love and peace who I once gave up on any hope that He would help me in my life. I wondered if He ever really existed. When I was greeted by Him, as I walked into Heaven through the clouds, my uncertainty was erased for good. He was smiling and waiting for me. I could not help but smile at Him and say, "You do exist." Jesus extended His arms as if He were waiting for me to walk over and hug Him. So, I did just that! Jesus said, "Welcome home. We have a lot of work to do."

Jesus pulled away from our hug and put His arm over my shoulder. He guided me forward with Him to our next stop: my life reviews. This took place in a golden room. This is also the place where I learned I had guides assisting me throughout my life. Jesus was one, and there were others: Archangel Michael, Mary, Jesus' mother, El Moyra, and St. Germain.

I once thought a life review was a fake projection of thought, but I was so wrong. My life review was very real.

Megan C Brown

I felt every feeling I have ever had in every moment and the feelings of the others involved in those occasions. What I had a hard time believing was how judgmental I once was.

Each started by telling me I had done well so far because I kept moving forward. As I watched my life play out on a movie screen with surprise every single moment of my existence up to that moment, I smiled, I cried, I laughed, I was visibly distressed, and I threw up. It was a myriad of feelings throughout the experience. I was even informed during this time of some things that were going to be happening when I went back to earth to finish out my life. They spoke to me about what was going to be emotionally difficult for me and then waited for my response. I said, "This too shall pass."

They all nodded their heads and said, "That is so." At this moment They were testing me to see how I would respond as the new me on earth. Did I understand what was being said? If I didn't understand and I said yes, they would know I was lying. There's no getting around being honest there.

What was constant was the support from my guides throughout. Each was attentive to my every need during this process. I was made to feel comfortable in a most uncomfortable situation to my human thought process.

It was time to get dressed in my Heaven attire after watching my life review. Archangel Michael took me into a golden room where three golden cherub Angels were in the air praying around me. They dressed me in a white robe I was required to wear while visiting. I was then handed a white stole. This stole was bordered with gold at the seams. The Angels helped dress me, placed the stole over my head, and properly positioned it. The top of the stole was over my right shoulder, and the bottom was

A Catalyst

unattached overlapping my left hip. On the bottom piece of material that overlapped the top piece was a purple emblem. The emblem was earth with seven flames emerging from it. This stole was an indicator I was visiting. With the palm of their hands facing me, a white beam of light shot out from their hands. They were cleansing me for the next visit that has become a personal turning point for me.

When the cherubs were finished, they left the room. Archangel Michael and I stood looking at each other. He was 6'7", had dark chocolate skin color, dark brown wavy hair that went to His shoulders, and beautiful hazel-colored eyes. His demeanor was peaceful and powerful all at once. He smiled at me and said, "Welcome home."

I humbly replied, "Hi. Thank you." I remember looking to the floor because I felt like crying. I couldn't believe the power of love I felt looking directly at me. It was intense.

Archangel Michael began, "I must cleanse you and protect you in this now. God has ordered Me to tattoo you in another fashion. It won't hurt. I promise. You will place your hands directly out to your side and look up when I tell you to. I will be tattooing your soul with Psalm 91. Are you familiar with it?"

"No," I said. "All of the catechism classes, confirmation, and masses I attended intermittently throughout my life have not prepared me for this moment. I do apologize for my ineptness."

"Worry not. I am not here to judge you. I am here to love you," Archangel Michael said with a sweet smile on His face. "Please place your hands out with your palms up and tilt your head back looking up to the center of the gold dome above you."

Megan C Brown

At this time, I wept softly as Archangel Michael recited Psalm 91 in a most powerful tone of voice. He invoked the power of love. I felt love looking at me in a way I did not know was possible. I felt a nurturing and warmth feeling during what He recounted with such ease. I felt the purest energy of relaxation and comfort as He spoke to me. I didn't want this moment to end. It was the best I had ever felt in my entire life. As Archangel Michael closed with the Aramaic version of Psalm 91, "…With the length of days I shall satisfy him and I shall show him my salvation," I fell to my knees and cried with my hands covering my face. At this time, Archangel Michael had moved close to me to place His hand on top of my head. I could feel a warm tingling and the sudden need to open my eyes. I took my hands down and kneeling before me was a glowing ball of white light surrounding Archangel Michael. I looked at His face and He smiled at me. He said, "Now psalm 91 will be your favorite psalm. You will turn to it during your dark moments. It will be felt by Me. I will never leave your side. I am your guide. Please think of Me often."

I could not help but smile at Him. I quietly said, "I will never forget this moment for as long as I live. Thank you." I bowed my head to Him.

Archangel Michael reached for my hands, and we stood together. I asked, "Can I give You a hug?"

He smiled at me and reached His arms around me as I reached mine around Him. For a few minutes, I hugged my arms around Him. This was an amazing moment. As Archangel Michael slowly pulled Himself away from me, He said, "We must now go to God's Temple. It is time."

"God's Temple?" I asked. "I'm going to meet God?"

"Yes, and Goddess, too," He responded. "There are many who are waiting to meet with you in this now. We

A Catalyst

must go." Archangel Michael took my right hand and led me out of this room to Jesus, Mary, St. Germain, and El Morya were waiting for me just outside of the room. Each smiled at me and turned as Archangel Michael and I walked with Them toward Synagogue. They guided me to a white Synagogue with a white dome in the center of the roof. I remember seeing two ornate small decks extending out from each side. Standing in each one was a solid gold Angel. The Angels themselves were draped in white and played golden trumpets to announce our approach.

Jesus opened the door and Mary entered first, followed by El Morya, then St. Germain, and finally Archangel Michael, me, and Jesus. I felt as though I was floating toward the golden table where Everyone was seated. I remember Jesus had pulled my golden chair out for me when I sat down.

The gloriousness of Everyone around me was jaw-dropping, to say the least. The colors were so vivid, and the gold was so gold, like nothing I'd ever seen before.

I saw multiple giant wings to my right as I approached the table to be seated. There was a feeling in this room that was like nothing I had ever felt before. There was a warmth I felt within, and it became my immediate mental and emotional security blanket. No matter what was said, I understood this feeling was for me.

The greatness of Who was before me took my breath away. I saw God sitting to my left at the head of the table. Jesus sat directly to the right hand of God. Seated to my immediate right was a straight line of Archangels down to Melchizedek and then Goddess. The Archangel line included giant cream-colored wings that began with Archangel Michael, then Archangel Gabriel, Archangel

Megan C Brown

Raphael, Archangel Ariel, Archangel Uriel, Archangel Nathanial, Archangel Raziel, Archangel Metatron, Archangel Haniel, Archangel Jeremiel, followed by more Archangels.

I had given up on the concept of God even existing. I didn't believe anything like this would be waiting for me in death.

God looked at me and said, "Welcome home. I am so glad to see you again. You have had a tough earth life, but you have done it well."

I said very humbly, "Thank you."

After saying thank you to God, the Congregation said in unison, "Blessings received."

When I heard, 'Blessings received,' I immediately understood. This is the highest energy in which to say thank you. They knew I was still shaking off the earth.

Then, suddenly in walked Gaius Julius Caesar, ruler of the Roman Empire approximately 100 BC, standing between God and Jesus at the table. He had a golden tan skin hue, with dark blonde hair that fell beautifully to about two inches above His shoulders. His physical body appeared to be in incredible physical shape. Due to my ignorance of proper protocol in a situation like this, I stood immediately and faced Him. I put my hands together in front of my chin and bowed before Him.

Caesar placed His hands on the table, and He began to speak to me, "I began as a Roman Magistrate, and rose to become Rome's first Emperor. History has written Me as being an evil dictator, but I stand before you now at God's table. As Rome's Emperor, I was considered sacrosanct. I was the first to conceive a constitutional right. I created an absolute law to prevail with My intent only as ruler of Rome. You know this law as being veto power. This official document was approved by Me only.

A Catalyst

I exercised the right as Emperor to decide an outcome because of this one law. The remaining laws were enforced and adhered to as an equal system. I created the first democratic state and government because of the disorder of the Roman Republic. My purpose was to achieve peace for the new Roman State. A unanimous vote declared My victory. Personal agendas I was unaware of resulted in my murder. "

I responded sincerely to Caesar's statement, "I will tell everyone Your truth, Caesar."

Caesar bowed His head and said, "Blessings received." Then He turned and walked around God to be seated at the open chair next to the left of Jesus' mother Mary who was seated to God's left side. I was thunderstruck by the power around me.

After listening to Julius Caesar, I had a question for God. "With all of the thousands of people dying today, how is it You are here with me?"

God replied, "I am an atom. I multiply My soul as many times as I need to."

I feel honored to be able to share how God and Goddess looked. God had a gentle smile displayed with a white beard and mustache, what appeared to be a dark, golden tan, and He wore a white robe with a gold stole that was adorned over His left shoulder. The Goddess was the most visibly stunning woman I had ever seen. She had a beautiful smile, a dark, golden tan, and was clothed in a white robe with a purple stole that was placed over Her right shoulder. She wore a crown on her head that had thirteen big chunks of amethyst delicately displayed meeting at a raised point in the center.

God began the conversation, "I bet you're wondering why all of these ascended masters,

Megan C Brown

Archangels, and saints are here at My table. Soon, they will reveal their truths for you."

I was numb as to how to feel by the power in front of me. I felt I was way out of my league.

The frequencies are so fast in Heaven. The more love, the faster and higher the frequency. When the frequencies are faster and higher, they radiate and tap into my ability as a being to receive everything given to me. This includes information I retain in my memory.

God continued, "Creation must be built upon the love that is prayer. To reprogram humanity is going to be done no matter what. With consistent repetition, results are created. The result of only love is love, whereby the rhythm that had occurred magnified it beyond the original intent. I'm talking about magnifying the feeling of love to create echoing, and a continuing effect of the echo to enhance the outcome through vibration. It's already in the works. The earth as you know it will change significantly by the year 2022. Humanity will be more compassionate, ninety percent of wars eradicated, people's priorities completely changed, religion will be understood, and more thought will go into an individual's daily life. There is unbridled love in Heaven being available on earth as well. Everyone must shift their thoughts to acceptance for all. Humans have created many rules about 'love.' Who you can love, and how you can love? There are no rules. Love is limitless. Being labeled as a homosexual, heterosexual, lesbian, transsexual, bisexual, transgender, or asexual are man-made stigmas. I think no more and no less of any of them than I do of you. You are all equal. You are all My creation. Those souls are more balanced in a yin and yang sense than you are. Monogamy is a choice. You must tell everyone I love all homosexuals, lesbians, transsexuals,

A Catalyst

bisexuals, transgenders, and everyone under the sun. I love no one less, and no one more. You can never fail when life is lived in love. Do not speak to another soul and ask for their thought about your thought. You are on a personal quest and mission for Me. You are all My perfection of love. You are each an example of excellence, exactness, and precision. There is nothing stronger than my intent of love. You will always prevail with your thoughts being in love. Do you have any questions for Me?" God closed.

"Why are You telling me about all of this?" I asked with sincerity.

"I am ordering you to write a book," God said.

My thought currently was, "Oh shit."

"Yes," God said, "Oh shit is right."

I quickly responded, "I am sorry Your Holiness for having used this language in Your presence. Will You forgive me?"

"Yes, my child I have already forgiven you. Those words mean nothing to Me. They are manmade. You were merely sharing your realization of where you are right now. Now you know I do know everything. Be careful what you wish for because I hear those, too."

"Oops," I joked aloud. Everyone at the table laughed.

The next person I remember was Goddess. She looked at me with love, "You have been living your life in fear up to this point. You are wasting your time. You need to be the woman and soul you are, or you are doing yourself a disservice, and the world a disservice."

While looking at Her I said, "Blessings received."

I humbly moved forward to the next ascended master sitting to Her right, White Eagle.

Megan C Brown

White Eagle was wearing a huge, beautiful, white-feathered headdress and his Native American attire.

White Eagle made it a point to tell me about the white feather and what it represents. "The white feather represents holiness, purity, and deep spirituality. When you find a white feather while you are outdoors, you should reflect on your life at that moment. Examine what you are doing. Are you doing, or being? Have you recognized the fullness of your soul, and who you are? You don't have to be part of a tribe to receive the blessing of the white feather. It applies to every soul on earth. This is a sign of unification."

White Eagle told me fifteen places in the world send out the highest frequencies of love that can be felt through the earth: Bora Bora, Australia, Hawaii, Easter Island, Japan, Bali, Key West, Brazil, Canada, Switzerland, Iceland, Egypt, Madagascar, Santorini, and New Guinea.

"Blessings received," I said, and I looked to my right.

Charan Singh spoke gently, "Just because some of your family members did not follow what I had written, does not mean what I had written was not with love. You chose to follow me, and you remember I came to you?"

"Yes," I said.

"You saw your past life with me, you saw the cows while I was initiating you. It did happen. It was us together. Continue to love. Just love. Being human is work. You are a work in progress. What truths I put forward were a list of simple rules to follow given to me by God to obtain more purity in the human form. You tried to follow vegetarianism, but years later resorted to eating meat again. You are still loved as you can see. Love is eternal," said Charan Singh.

I quietly said, "Blessings received."

A Catalyst

The next person I spoke to was Paramahansa Yogananda. He smiled at me and said, "You knew of Me as well when you were young. You were at the Self Realization Center in Malibu. You loved it there and didn't understand My teachings and purpose in life then. You felt very peaceful there. You knew the intentions of the place, and having it built was for good and for the highest vibration of love to be felt. You felt as if others were more advanced than you. What you will come to realize, is you, and the rest are working at different speeds. It is just how it should be."

I looked into Yogananda's eyes and said, "Blessings received."

I moved forward to the next seat. I was greeted with a smile by Mahatma Gandhi. He began, "Peace has always been met with resistance. The peace you will propose will include freedom from strife for everyone. Have patience. Holding space for peace is not easy. Your mission will include every one of us here. Just because We are in Heaven does not mean We have stopped working for peace. My hand is at your back assisting you forward always."

"Blessings received," I said. I moved forward to the next chair. I was greeted by a smile from a man with dark brown skin, dark brown slicked back hair, and dressed in a silk, golden robe, adorned with seven thick gold chains covering His chest. He wore black-rimmed glasses over His eyes, and golden, silk-roped sandals. Prophet Muhammad Ibn 'Abd Allah Ibn Abd al-Muttalib was born April 26th, 319 A.D., in Mecca, and died June 8th, 363 AD.

Prophet Muhammad was and still is a revered and highly regarded religious leader. Prophet Muhammad created and unified Arabia, with a religious denomination, Islam. Prophet Muhammad declared only peace. It was His mission to tell all who would listen, to choose the path of least resistance. Peace for all was His mission.

He said, "I am someone you are not familiar with. It matters not. I am introducing Myself to you now. My message of peace has been obstructed by greed. You are to put everything I say to you in your book. Do not detract. I too will have My hand at your back to assist you forward."

"Blessings received," I said softly.

The next ascended master was a beautiful charcoal black-skinned woman. "I am Kali," She said. "All of the pain you have lived through, I was there. I will continue to help you so you may now serve your highest purpose."

"Blessings received," I said quietly.

Next, I remember walking up to God who looked at me and said, "Picture yourself sitting in the driver's seat of your car. You choose which road you will be taking, and how you want to drive. Just remember I am always the passenger next to you. I know what will happen, but it is not My job to tell you, or you will miss the lesson. Just know I am always with you. Your choices are My gift to you."

"Blessings received," I said. I looked at God straight in His eyes. I asked Him respectfully, with humor attached, "Can I touch Your cheek?"

God said, "Yes."

I reached out and touched His left cheek gently. Then I smiled and said, "Now I can tell people I have touched the face of God."

God said, "You've been here a day. Have you learned anything?"

"Yes," I said softly.

A Catalyst

"What?" He asked.

"I have learned about a love I have never heard of or felt before. I have learned others here were not immune to pain. I have learned I was living in fear unnecessarily. There is nothing to fear," I responded.

"You have been paying attention," God said softly with a comforting smile. "I am calling you to the task."

"You are?" I questioned.

"Yes," God said.

"Okay. What do You want me to do?" I asked.

"I want you to tell everyone what you saw here. I want you to tell everyone why you are now a believer. You must tell them about everything you have seen. Please include everything that makes you feel uncomfortable about your Heaven experience as well," God instructed.

"It makes me nervous to talk about Prophet Muhammad, Jesus, Paramahansa Yogananda, and Quan Yin in the same book," I answered.

"Yes, but I am not asking you to feel comfortable with what I am telling you. I am ordering you to feel uncertainty, and at the same time feel certain about our conversation here. Do you have any questions?" God asked.

"No," I said.

God stood before me. He put both of His hands on my shoulders and said, "I promise I will not leave you. I promise." God leaned forward and kissed my forehead.

I bowed my head before Him and cried, "I don't want to fuck this up. This is like a job interview I have never been on before." After saying what I said about the job interview, I began to laugh. Then God laughed with me. God smiled comfortingly again and said softly, "I have faith. I am hiring a pro." God sat back down in His chair and ordered me to go back and sit in mine.

I remember getting up from my chair again at God's table and walking over to a tall wooden door I had not seen yet. This door represented the last feeling of the earth. With my hand on the door, I paused for a moment. I turned back and looked at everyone at the table and said, "You mean if I go through this door I don't have to go back?"

In unison, they said with a smile on Their faces, "Yes."

"Well, I can't go now after all of the time You spent pouring Your hearts out to me. I'm feeling a tinge of Catholic guilt surfacing," I said while laughing. Everyone laughed, and I went back to the table and sat down.

God began speaking again, "Theories of thirteen crystal skulls are surfacing. The skulls are affiliated with the Mayan civilization. Each skull is pre-programmed with information of 26,000 years. The master plan for the current 26,000 years began December 22nd, 2012. The current 26,000, years is pre-programmed in a black obsidian skull that resides on the outskirts of Baghdad, Iraq, in the Euphrates River. Scientists will be able to find it. It will be found. When the scientists hold it, they are to listen and note what they hear. Powerful information consisting of Saudi Arabia's transformation will be heard from this skull. A purification of their current cultural belief started in July 2007. The black obsidian skull holds the assurance of new world order for the Middle East. Drastic changes to include world alliance will be achieved. Peace will prevail as world uniformity. Strife throughout the Middle East will come to an end. A forced change will be felt by all the earth. Previous understanding of how the world runs changed on

A Catalyst

December 22nd, 2012. The Middle East will be setting the precedence of leadership in all ways."

Archangel Uriel began, "I am a powerful force lighting the way to freedom from uncertainty. I will enlighten the universe with understanding and peace. It is My mission to always incorporate pure understanding."

Archangel Ariel spoke softly, "I am the keeper of light for love. I am also the destroyer of evil and the underworld. I work closely with Archangel Michael."

Archangel Michael stated, "I will protect every all serving love. You have felt my energy. Do you doubt me?"

I immediately said, "Absolutely not. I will never doubt any of you again. I am a new woman because of this experience. You have made me listen very closely. Blessings received."

God said, "I am waiting for your book to be finished. Will you mention your newfound love for Me?"

Without a pause, I said, "I will even confess to never having believed in You. Now I do and I am a true believer. Blessings received for Your patience with me, God. I know I am a handful."

Everyone at the table laughed at my having attempted to make God smile. I succeeded.

Jesus said, "Seeing as how confessions are at hand, I must say I have never been greeted how you greeted Me. Do you believe I exist now?"

"Without a doubt," I said. "I will start praying to You and put a cross up in my house."

Jesus just smiled at me with absolute acceptance. He put His right hand on my shoulder and patted it lovingly.

Prophet Muhammad spoke up lovingly and said, "I will always be with you. What do you think about that?"

Megan C Brown

With my witty self, I said, "Do I have a choice?" Thankfully, my playful response was well received by the entire congregation, including Prophet Muhammad, as I had intended it. "I love You, Prophet Muhammad. I do not know Your power on earth, but I have felt Your power as I stood before You. Love is all I have felt from You. Blessings received."

White Eagle said, "I have loved you throughout your current earth life. Please let it comfort you to know I will continue to do so."

I asked White Eagle, "My current earth life? What do you mean by that?"

White Eagle answered, "You have been incarnated many times. I have loved you from Heaven through many lives."

I responded, "Incarnation exists?"

The entire table responded in unison, "Yes."

"Oh my God," I said not remembering I was sitting with God. It was a knee-jerk human response.

"I am right here," God answered. Again, the entire table laughed with joy.

I said with a huge smile, "That's right You are. Oh my God. I can make sense-making that statement now. Incredible. "I continued to laugh with everyone.

As the laughter began to die down, a serious voice spoke, "I hate to ruin the mood, but I am not a joke teller. I appreciate so very much this time with laughter. It has been quite refreshing. My name is Archimedes. I am a mathematician and scientist. I have tried to assist you in both classes, but they are not your forte."

"Did you have to out me?" I said quickly with a smile to which Archimedes laughed again.

"I have been asked to join you here to give to you detailed information about the science of love. God has

176

A Catalyst

asked Me to meet with you while you are here. I am happy to do so," Archimedes said respectfully.

I responded, "I promise I will be a better student. Blessings received for Your time, Archimedes."

Suddenly another male voice spoke. It was Hippocrates. He said, "I am Hippocrates. God has asked Me to meet with you as well. I know you have not attended medical school either, but thankfully it is not a requirement for the book God has asked you to write."

Suddenly Kali spoke again, "I have loved you through the past three thousand years. I am with you always. I never leave your side."

I quickly replied, "You are the most beautiful woman I have ever seen. Your teeth are perfect. Your eyes are glowing love. How is this possible?"

Kali said, "I love you. My eyes have only love for you."

I lovingly replied, "Blessings received. Please do not ever stop loving me. When I come back again, I hope You still look at me in this way. I will never forget You."

Archangel Gabriel spoke up, "I have loved you through your toughest times on earth and I gave you the voice to speak during those times when you felt voiceless."

I said softly, "I know the times You speak of well. I cannot forget them. Blessings received for never having left me. I love You."

"I love you, too," Archangel Gabriel said.

God said, "You have much love here, Megan. How does it feel to know you are loved here?"

I humbly replied, "Oh God, I cannot thank You enough for allowing me to be graced by Your presence and all who are here with me. I have never felt more fulfilled in my entire life. Well, this one anyway. I do not remember my other lives. Blessings received."

God responded, "You are so welcome. As you can see you are so welcome here. Please enjoy your stay with Us, but know that you will be attending violin classes, medical classes with Hippocrates, and science and math classes with Archimedes. I have also arranged music history classes for you with Johann Sebastian Bach and Wolfgang Amadeus Mozart. Don't worry, you will not be receiving piano lessons. You will also be watching the demise of civilizations with Jesus. You believe in Him now, right?"

I smiled, "Yes Father, I am a true believer."

"Good," God replied. "If you have any questions, please let them be known to Archangel Michael. He will be leading you through your experience while you are here visiting Us in Heaven. Do you have any questions in this now for Me?"

"I do," I said politely, "May I ask Archangel Michael questions as they come up, or do I have to ask You?"

God said, "Please ask Him anything you desire. Think of Me as the backup guy just in case anyone here needs more help with you."

"I have a feeling I am going to require a lot of help. I already blew it with psalm 91, and I have never read the Bible," I replied.

God said, "Worry not. Those are not requirements to get into Heaven. You are here, aren't you?"

"Yes, I am, and I don't want to leave," I replied.

"Yes, well, it is not your time to come home to Heaven. We have work for you to do on earth. Will you please assist Me on earth?" God asked.

A Catalyst

"Anything for You, Father. I am so honored. What if humanity doesn't believe my story? What should I do?" I asked.

God stated, "It is not for you to do your work with the expectations of anyone. Do you understand this? I am only asking you to write your truths of Heaven within your experience here. You are a part of well-laid plans by Me to divert the eyes, ears, and actions of humanity from evil. I am ordering you to write your book about love as it has never been done before. Will you do this for Me knowing all of humanity may not believe you?"

"Yes," I said without hesitation.

"Blessings received," God answered.

Currently every eye at the table was on me and God. Not one soul sitting around me moved while God spoke to me. It was as quiet as a church mouse. Then suddenly, a gentle voice spoke up. It was Goddess and She said, "We are all with you at all times. We love you, Megan. You have nothing to fear."

I had to ask courteously, "Goddess how is it all of You will love me and I didn't even believe in any of You? Please forgive me, but I thought you were a metaphorical creation for woman's rights."

Again, the table was silent as each waited for Goddess to respond. She said, "Megan, I only love. I cannot judge your thoughts and feelings. I can love you through them. My love is not conditioned to your beliefs."

"Oh, thank God," I responded to Goddess. At this time, I looked over at God and said, "Another earth term. You are so popular, God. I just wish everyone believed what they were saying." Again, the entire congregation laughed, including God.

Megan C Brown

"Some do and some don't," God said while laughing.

I said, "Seeing as how I am confessing everything to all of You, Jesus, you're next. Okay, I am guilty of having said, 'Oh Jesus,' but I'm not calling out for You. I am just pissed off. Yes, I am even guilty of having said, 'Jesus Christ,' again in anger. Jesus, will You forgive me for this?"

Jesus was smiling and said, "Yes, I forgive you. Do you think I haven't heard that before? I am popular in angered responses. I wonder why?"

"I do not know, Jesus," I said, "but can You imagine if You just appeared next to every person who said that and said, 'Yes. How can I help you?'"

Again, everyone at the table was laughing. It felt so good to laugh with all these incredibly powerful beings. What I had learned in catechism classes and the Catholic Church did not include humor. I also thought making it into Heaven would be a stretch for me because I had quit going to church. Now I am relieved. Not only does God, Jesus, Archangel Michael, and Prophet Muhammad have a sense of humor, but I have already been told I will be going back. The thought of this makes my soul smile.

When the laughter softened, my attention was brought to another Archangel. It is awesome to have been spoken to by These beautiful beings who look human. Appearing human and having giant cream-colored feathered wings extending up over Their heads about two feet and the bottom of the wings touching the floor as They sat at the table. Imagine multiple Archangels sitting side by side at God's golden table. Each was physically beautiful. Archangel Nathaniel began, "My name is Archangel Nathaniel. I am here to help you open the invisible doors within you to your deepest dreams and

A Catalyst

desires. When you have been silent privately pondering the meaning of your life, you already knew it was to write a book. Is this true?"

"Yes," I said softly. "When I was nineteen, I wrote a story that included Heaven."

"Why did you not pursue this as your life purpose?" Archangel Nathaniel asked me gently.

"Because I thought of it as being a slice of pie in the sky as my grandfather used to say to me. It didn't mean anything. It was just a personal dream."

"Where is that personal dream now?" Archangel Nathaniel asked.

"It is inside a closet in my home," I replied.

"Do you think you will ever pull it out of the closet and bring it to life as you have dreamt?" He wondered aloud.

"I forgot all about it. Now that I am being ordered to write this book, I guess it would be the best time to bring that story in my closet to life."

"Please do so. It was brilliant," Archangel Nathaniel stated.

"Well, from Your mouth to God's ears! There is another earth saying for You God. I wish You could be my agent on earth, Archangel Nathaniel," I said.

"I am," Archangel Nathaniel responded. "I am just one of your many agents here in Heaven. I am curious. Who do you think has more pull? Heaven, or a singular agent on earth?"

"I don't know how it works here, so I do not have an answer for You," I said respectfully.

"FYI, we hold the power, Megan. Nothing is more powerful than God's will," Archangel Nathaniel said.

At this time, another beautiful voice to the right of Archangel Nathaniel spoke up. It was Archangel Haniel, a beautiful female with long wavy blonde hair. She represents victory and intuition. Archangel Haniel said, "I am your leader to yourself. I will always remind you to listen to your gut feelings. This is your term for intuition. Please begin to pray when you go back. Praying will assist you in making your intuition stronger. When you pray, you are connecting to your soul self. An alignment of Divine love is happening. Please let this be known in your book."

I respectfully responded, "I will. Blessings received. May I compliment You?"

Archangel Haniel smiled at me and said, "Please do so."

"You are so beautiful as well. Why is everyone in Heaven so beautiful?" I asked sincerely.

"Blessings received," Archangel Haniel said. "We are love. Love is a most beautiful being, isn't it?"

"Yes," I said softly. "I wish I could see love like all of You in human form."

God declared, "You do. You must accept each human as the individual love vessel each is. Then you will view each as the beauty they are."

When God said this, He gave me the key to the kingdom within me. To accept everyone is my gift to the world and myself.

Goddess said, "Acceptance is synonymous with love, Megan."

Then, as if rehearsed, the entire congregation spoke in unison, "Acceptance is synonymous with love."

"You have accepted Us," Goddess said. "You have no reservations about who We are. How does what I say feel to you?"

"Amazing," I responded.

A Catalyst

"It is with great pleasure We meet with you in this now. You are one of many who will be helping Us put the word out about love," Goddess said.

I began, "I am truly honored to be here with You and everyone at this table. I am in awe of the greatness that exists in Heaven. I once thought it was all just a bunch of made-up stories. I am so sorry I did not believe."

God asked me, "Do you believe right now?"

"Yes. Without a doubt," I said.

Archangel Michael was sitting up straight in His chair to my immediate right. His wings were glowing a golden hue. He said, "We have welcomed you home for a reason. This experience was already written in the timeline."

I listened intently. I waited for a moment to hear more, but Archangel Michael stopped. I waited another moment in case Someone else was going to speak, but no one spoke up. I politely asked, "What is the timeline? I've never heard of it before. Is this something taught in the Catholic Church?"

Archangel Michael stated, "The timeline is not known on earth at this time. You must introduce it in your book. This book you will write is a puzzle piece of sorts. There is an exact line drawn in a gold tablet that was created by God. Each line indicates a date in time with a symbol next to it. Each symbol is a human form with its name and description of love being presented to the world. Sometimes the same human form is indicated more than once. Your soul purpose is, now known to you. Every soul is established in This timeline I speak of, but not every soul chooses to serve love. The soul position then becomes erased. I speak of a fluctuation of love's energy. The intent is written, but a human's choice can and does alter the power of love. You see Us here at the table? We have all served as loves symbol. We continue to serve as a love symbol. Our power is greater than ever on this planet because We only serve love. The frequency speed of love is currently not understood on earth. How can one better life without understanding? We are giving you the omnipotent ingredient. Love. You will receive lessons with Archimedes and Hippocrates who will Each explain the scientific equations of love. The mathematical quotients must be implemented in the earth's daily living for the reversal of negativity to take place. There is no other way to world peace. One must understand love's strategy."

God declared, "I am the producer, but you must be the writer and director on earth. Will you do this for Me?"

"Yes," I said, "But I must tell you that I was not very good in English class. I do not want to fail You, God."

God replied, "You will not fail writing your book. We will all make sure you understand the classes you will be attending here in Heaven. Your understanding will bring into fruition the creation of beauty on the pages you fill."

Goddess stated, "I love everyone, Megan. I want you to make this known in your book."

"I will. I promise," I responded.

Jesus said, "We all have faith in you. We do not meet at God's table at the end of anyone's life. A soul is always met by Me, and everyone's guides. We are here with you because We are all guiding you now. We have been asked to introduce Ourselves to you and tell you your soul purpose. Once We have finished with this meeting, we are obligated to court you through the rest of your visit here in Heaven. We will be assisting you through the rest of your earth life. When you return, we will meet with you like this once again. Do you have any questions?"

A Catalyst

I was so curious currently. How could I not be? Yet, I was also nervous. It became obvious to me how serious the mission was God was ordering me to write in my book. All the incredibly powerful beings surrounding me Each with a message for me to put in the book. I did not want to mess this up. "Not at this time," I softly responded.

God announced, "It is in this time you will be brought to your dwelling place during your visit here in Heaven. Archangel Michael will assist you in every all way. Please stay focused on your classes but be prepared for some fun while you are here."

At this time, everyone at the table stood up and looked at me. All at once, I heard, "Blessings received." Each soul walked around the table to me and hugged me. Seventy-five hugs later I was guided by Archangel Michael out of Synagogue.

I remember entering a tent. It was royal purple and white in color with gold thread lining the edges. My first meeting was with Jesus who entered the tent and sat in the big white chair. Archangel Michael and I sat on the white couch. Jesus began a discussion regarding sadness associated with having been wronged. As He explained His frustration in one line, He looked at me and asked me to share one of mine. Well, I didn't have only one frustration I had many.

I looked at Jesus and began with my being sad about not having been guided in any way. I expressed my frustration at having been ignored in my life.

Jesus looked at me and asked, "What is upsetting you, Megan?"

I looked at Him while sitting speechless for a moment before Him. Finally, I said, "I have to learn to forgive."

Jesus smiled and acknowledged, "That is so."

I sat quietly looking down at the floor for a moment. I looked back up at Jesus and said, "Blessings received. Jesus You just told me I am responsible for healing myself, didn't You?"

Jesus smiled, "That is so. How do you choose to live the rest of your life?"

"Well, now You've put a different spin on everything. You have handed the ball back to me haven't You Jesus?" I responded.

"Yes. How do you want to play ball now?" Jesus smiled.

He made so much sense it took me a moment to respond without crying. "I have a choice to walk away and let go of the pain, forgive, or forgive and try to reconnect."

"I think you've got the idea," Jesus said with a smile. "Describe to me how pain feels to you."

"Well, that's a question I've never been asked before," I responded. I thought about it for a moment. "Pain takes over my thoughts. It dictates how I respond to situations. I don't know how to let it go."

"Would you like Me to guide you to a new way of thinking?" Jesus asked.

"Yes," I replied.

"Think about your life. It has already happened. You are in control of your life now," Jesus said gently.

"I am," I responded softly.

"Yes. You can also ask for assistance from Me, Archangel Michael, God, and many Others. We want to help you, Megan," Jesus smiled.

I thought about what Jesus was pointing out to me for a moment. I looked down to the floor and began to put pain in perspective. I had a moment of precision when the

A Catalyst

pain began to take form in my mind. Each pain has an origin with my feelings and emotions attached to them. My response is my choice and is my power. Suddenly I looked up at Jesus to share my light bulb moment with him, "Jesus I know when each pain began and what happened in each situation. I am the only one who can determine how long the pain will reside in my mind. Of course, this is a lot easier said than done."

Jesus smiled at me and said, "Is there more you would like to share with Me?"

"Yes. I have been a dysfunctional protective mother to my children's pain, feelings, and emotion. Jesus, I have ignored these children of mine. I turned away from painful feelings and emotions because I did not know how to talk to them. I acted like a victim to all of them. This makes me responsible for out-of-control behavior inside of me, and how I interact with others. Oh shit. What a mess. These children have grown up inside of me, so I've provided them with housing. I do not know how to get these metaphorical kids to move out. What do I do?" I said with a tinge of unease.

Jesus smiled again and asked me, "Did you name your metaphorical children?"

"Jesus, I did not know the pain was my child who needed to be nurtured and cared for," I stated.

"If you could give your metaphorical child pain, a name, what would it be?" Jesus asked me.

"I would name my pain Love," I said gently with a smile.

"Why?" Jesus asked.

I began, "I have not been a recipient of a lot of love. I am visiting a place where I can only feel love. I feel like a walking billboard of pain. Yet, when I sat in Synagogue with You, God, and the rest, You Each called me by my name. Pain is a part of me but separate from whom I want to be. The pain must be recognized by, me, as having a purpose. I want to integrate love into my daily life, so I will name my metaphorical child, Love.

"That's beautiful Megan," Jesus remarked. "What is your metaphorical child Love's purpose for your future?"

Again, I looked down at the floor and thought about His question for a moment. I looked back up at Him and said, "She is my protector."

"What does that mean, Megan?" Jesus asked.

I began, "I know where Love's pain happened."

Jesus asked me, "What happened to Love in each painful circumstance?"

"My serenity was taken from me," I said softly and began to cry. After a few moments, I continued, "Love kept asking me why, but I couldn't hear her question."

Jesus asked me, "Why?"

"Because I felt powerless and out of control. To some degree, I was out of control because of my age. When I was a young adult my Love displayed anger to protect the deepest sadness I did not want to speak to. I did not know I had the power to create a new dialogue with Love inside of me. Love is who I am. Love is my teacher," I said.

"That is so," Jesus confirmed with His beautiful smile. "There is something more about love I would like to inform you of. Love does not require you to keep pain housed in your mind. Being that a soul is a computer chip holding every groove of every record from every incarnation, you are authorized by God, Goddess, and all of Us who serve love to keep your records in a personal museum. When the surface of your pain takes a moment to step outside of your feeling in the moment. You are your historian. You must decide how to display your life. Will you separate it into three-year increments? Each section is symbolic of who you are. Being that everyone's reality is an extensive amount of information in one's memory bank, all of Us in Heaven ask you to lighten our mental load. We want you to bring your mind to everlasting freedom. How do you want to begin your new eternal interaction with your soul?"

"Jesus, I feel like I've been the passenger on a train, and now I feel as though I'm listening to the tracks for the first time. I've been letting a conductor take me on a ride instead of me being my conductor. I must switch tracks and continue into the rise of my dawn. I want to comfort Love who is inside of me. She will no longer be avoided by me because she has tremendous significance. Without Love, my soul could not exist. Because of Love, I have an eternal blueprint to add on to," I said.

"Your perception is an exquisite layout," Jesus stated.

"Blessings received," I said.

"Are you going to ask your soul creations to move into your museum?" Jesus inquired.

"Only the pain. I will honor each by displaying them as lessons in my classroom of life. Without them, I would be dull and uninformed. They've taught me what happiness is," I said.

"You have been a successful student, Megan. You understand thoroughly Heaven's mission for every soul to arrive at their new permanent residence called, ETERNAL SERENITY," Jesus smiled.

At this time Archangel Michael began to speak, "In April of 1842, a white, thirty-year-old man went into the grocery store to get something to eat. As he was standing in line, a black woman entered the store with her mother. Because he was the town mayor, he was curious to see who was entering through the door. The beautiful black woman caught his eye. He discreetly watched her follow her mother in. He felt a love gush in the center of his chest when he looked at her. He continued to wait for his sandwich and occasionally checked the location of the two women. When the butcher had finished the mayor's sandwich, he handed it to him followed by polite formalities. The mayor obtained his sandwich and began to leave the store. After polite attention, to those he recognized, he exited the store.

Continuing across the street, he began to eat his sandwich and wait for the two women to leave the store. When he finished, there was no reason to continue standing where he was. There was a trashcan located in front of the store. He methodically approached the store again to throw away his trash. As he got closer, the two women exited the store. He followed them in the most unassuming way. They happened to be walking in the direction of the mayor's home. The mayor followed them. When they were far enough out of town, the mayor called for the two women to take them by surprise. They both stopped and stared a serious look at him. Being that this was taking place in Mississippi, and it was the mayor asking them to stop, they complied.

As he approached them, he was trying to quickly determine what to say. He smiled at them and asked them if they would join him on his walk back home. He added being a bachelor and working, as the town mayor, did not allow him time to properly keep his home in order. The ladies smiled at him, and quietly followed him to his home.

Once inside, the mayor asked them both to be seated and make themselves comfortable in the living room. They smiled politely and awkwardly sat down.

A Catalyst

The mayor sat across from both in another chair. He began to explain he had lied to them. He wanted them to feel comfortable coming into his home. The older mother was visibly upset and began to quietly express to him what she was thinking. To which he interrupted her and apologized again. He politely asked if she was the younger woman's mother. She gave a nod. He looked down for a moment, and then looked back up at her.

He explained the story of standing waiting for his sandwich at the deli when he heard the door of the store open. He told the mother when he looked at her daughter, he felt she was the most beautiful woman he had ever seen. The mother stared at him for a moment as if looking into his soul. To which she responded, "Why would you, the mayor, risk everything to meet my daughter?"

He gently replied, "I am a romantic at heart. I've never felt this way before, and I would like to pursue an honest relationship with your daughter. Providing you can forgive me for how it has started."

The mother quickly replied, "How do you plan to have a relationship with my black daughter in Mississippi?"

"Privately," he remarked.

Again, the mother stared at the mayor and her daughter who was looking at her mother. Curious as to how she was going to respond to him. She asked her daughter, "What do you want?"

"He seems gentle, and he's cute," the woman observed.

Her mother sat for a moment before she responded. "You better be serious mister. This is my only child."

"I am only serious, ma'am," replied the mayor.

The mayor continued looking at the mother and invited both to stay for dinner. He assured them he had no intention of asking them to cook for him. He asked them to follow him into the kitchen and be seated. He poured the mother a shot of whiskey, handed it to her. She tossed it back immediately. She looked at him, smiled, and asked for another. He smiled at her, picked up her glass, and poured her one more. She nursed this one. The mayor handed her daughter a glass of tea. The daughter smiled at him and thanked him. The beauty of her smile captured him. He continued putting together a dinner for all of them. The conversation was effortless for each of them.

About a half-hour after dinner was finished, he insisted on walking them home. Both were surprised by his courtesy.

Three-quarters of a mile down the road, all continued to the ladies living accommodations in a barn. The mayor quietly thanked them for staying for dinner and invited them back for dinner at five o'clock the following evening. He assured them he would walk them home again. The ladies smiled and accepted his invitation. They turned around and walked back to their lodging. He stood and watched, making sure they entered safely. When they did, he started back for his home.

The second dinner was enjoyable for all three of them. The mayor shared his family photos with them and told stories of his childhood. Both mother and daughter shared funny stories about their childhoods as well. The evening was pleasant and comfortable. Before it got too late, the mayor walked them back to their residence. Again, he invited them for dinner the following evening with one stipulation: the mother had to agree to cook dinner, but with the understanding that he considered her a friend. He promised a wonderful surprise for both

A Catalyst

at the next dinner. All were smiling. The mayor asked politely if he could give the smitten woman a kiss goodnight. She smiled and nodded. He leaned forward and slowly kissed her cheek. He pulled back. Both smiled at one another. She turned around, tugged at her mother's arm, and they walked toward their dwelling. When they entered safely, he turned around and headed for home.

The mayor was inwardly nervous when the ladies entered his home for the third dinner. He made them feel welcome, brought them both a glass of tea, placed a plate of muffins on the table, and told them to help themselves. They talked casually for a while, and the mayor shifted the conversation to a more serious tone. He looked into the mother's eyes and informed her, "I am in love with your daughter."

"My daughter feels the same way about you," she smiled.

He smiled at her daughter and stated, "I'm so happy you feel the same way." He got out of his chair and knelt on both knees in front of the daughter. He pulled a gold ring out of his pocket and look into her eyes. "I want you to be my wife. Will you be my wife?"

The woman's eyes became wider with surprise. Her hands were in front of her mouth, and she nodded. He reached for her wedding finger and placed the ring on it. She leaned forward with excitement and kissed him respectfully in front of her mother. He stood to his feet and reached for his soon-to-be wife's hand. When she stood, they both hugged for a moment. Her mother had tears of happiness in her eyes.

The mayor turned to a drawer and pulled out a Bible. He handed it to the mother and asked her to read her favorite passage. He led them into the guest bedroom where he had drawn the shades for privacy. He had a beautiful, simple white dress lying across the bed. "Would you be willing to marry me right now?" the mayor asked.

She nodded excitedly, and her mother smiled at him. He left the room and closed the door gently behind him. The mayor went to his room and changed into a suit. He put a piece of paper in his pocket and left his bedroom to see if they were ready. At the end of the hallway, he noticed the door was open.

Entering the room, he saw the most beautiful woman he had ever seen. He smiled at her while taking her hand, to help her stand before him. He looked at her mother and asked softly, "Will you please read your favorite passage? Then I would like to read what I have written."

"Yes," the mother smiled and stood to her feet as well. She became the pastor for this ceremony. When she finished, she gently closed the Bible and held it close to her chest.

The mayor looked into his bride's eyes. He pulled the piece of paper out of his pocket and read his pledges to her. "Will you be my wife?" he asked.

"Yes," she smiled. "Will you promise to be my husband forever?" she said in the most loving voice.

"Yes," he whispered. He leaned forward and kissed her. When the mayor finished kissing his bride, he turned to look at his new mother-in-law. "I promise to obey and take care of your daughter." He reached forward to hug her and say, "Thank you."

"Good luck," she joked. All of them laughed. "This is when I leave to make dinner," she smiled and left the bedroom.

The mayor and his wife smiled at one another as the bedroom door shut. For a respectable amount of time, they consummated their marriage.

A Catalyst

For the next seventeen years, they were secretly and happily married. The mayor built a secret home under his existing one for him and his wife to live freely.

When she went to visit her mother, she took her wedding band off and exited the house while it was still dark out. She always returned home when it was dark so no one could see her enter what others viewed as being the mayor's home.

One night the mayor waited patiently for his wife, but she never came home.

The next day he visited in the morning to her mother's home. He kept knocking until she came to the door. He entered shaking and began to cry. "She didn't come home."

"What?" the mother cried. The mayor reached out and pulled his mother-in-law toward him. They both wept for hours.

His mother-in-law passed away within six months due to the pain of her daughter being gone. The mayor began to keep a journal about his private pains. He could turn to no one and kept up appearances of being a lifelong, hard-working bachelor. His fixed position within the government.

It was three years later while journaling one night when he decided to turn his pain into a radical stance. First, he had to find a white wife. One who would help launch his next career. Within three months he was married in a very public, Christian wedding.

During his silent journaling, he connected to his soul purpose. His first marriage had to be confidential, and so too did the motivation for his career change. Having felt powerless in protecting his true love, he became determined to honor her publicly. He created and committed to his plan to abolish slavery.

Megan C Brown

In 1859, Abraham Lincoln became the 16th President of the United States of America. His secret marriage to a black woman was the impetus in his running for President. The perfection of love was ripped away from him because of her skin color. He knew by limiting how one was permitted to love, would ultimately limit the expansion of humanity.

His strategy for introducing equality to blacks would not be accessible if it were introduced as allowing one to love whoever one wanted. He recognized equality for all people had to be introduced covertly. His hope in launching the idea of accepting the difference of skin color would eventually unveil the next development within humanity. He knew the only way to remove an obstacle in obtaining this dream was to be in the White House. Abraham Lincoln's unforeseen heartache was the advancement our United States of America needed.

There is inaccurate information provided for us regarding how he served before working in the White House. President Lincoln's personal life was only private. The one exception was his wedding to Mary Todd."

Archangel Michael ended His story. I was quietly crying. My mind began to comprehend the invisible power our president wielded with such skill. His canvas of excruciating sorrow covering his heart was palpable.

After a few moments, President Abraham Lincoln walked into the tent. A golden chair appeared next to Jesus. I was taken by surprise, to say the least, and I put my hands over my nose and mouth as my involuntary reaction. President Lincoln was wearing a navy-blue suit, a white collared shirt with a plain, navy blue tie, and a pair of loafers on his feet. He looked at me, smiled, and began, "I understand God has new plans for the world.

A Catalyst

He has asked me to come and share with you more of My story."

I was crying still seated on the couch next to Archangel Michael because I did not have the strength to stand after hearing his love story. I wanted to fall to the floor. "I am honored to be in your presence, Mr. President."

President Lincoln smiled and replied, "I am honored to be in your presence. You are being given a task that has never been done before. A long visit in Heaven, and personal meetings with some of us."

I asked politely, "God doesn't give this information to everyone?"

"Never," President Lincoln said quietly. "I would like to speak to you in this now about the 13th, 14th, and 15th Amendments. The United States has stated in history books many untruths regarding my presidency. I am not being asked to make all the truths be known. It is appropriate for you to hear a specific truth regarding my reality while serving my country as president."

President Lincoln crossed his legs, placing his elbows on the arms of the chair, and linking his hands together. His relaxed demeanor seemed to be so gentle. "I would like to make very clear to earth how difficult it was for me to get the 13th, 14th and 15th Amendments passed. It is interesting to see how many individuals have included their names in each of these laws. Megan, I had no support. When I introduced the idea of freeing slaves and the details of each Amendment, I could have heard a mouse. I felt as if they were deciding where to lynch me. I stood before them with self-respect, and I kept repeating my internal dialogue, 'I am safe,' repeatedly as I looked at each of them in their eyes. It was important for me to connect in a subdued manner and be in control of this incredibly significant appearance. I knew this was going to be immediate, make it or break it an occasion. I would not get another chance at introducing the Amendments again." President Lincoln paused for a moment and looked down at the floor. When he looked back up at me, he had a tear rolling down his cheek. He softly spoke again, "After I entered Heaven, I could find out what happened to my wife. She had been raped, beaten, and mutilated because she was black. She was also pregnant with our first child. The daughter we had dreamed of having." President Lincoln looked back down at the floor. Tears were simultaneously streaming down his cheeks.

I was crying quietly as I looked down at the floor as well. I was saddened so deeply by his story. This sadness had a new plateau all by itself.

After a few minutes, President Lincoln continued, "When I stood before congress, I had no end to our love story. I had only a private obligation to honor her and make others do the same. I was determined, to be heard, and not fail my goal. All but two of the men I addressed agreed with me. It was a human right, not a right based upon the color of skin to enjoy the freedoms of the United States of America. If I had the power, to have made the 13th, 14th, and 15th Amendments globally accepted, I would have. No one deserves to feel less than because of their skin color. It was the man who created the story of whom to hate, not God."

I felt morally beholden to respond to this great leader sitting before me. I did not have the strength to speak without crying, so I whispered my thoughts while I looked directly into his eyes. "Blessings received for your bravery. Sir, you have enlightened me with a new definition for the word honor. Your nobility shined so brightly for humanity in creating the Amendments. How

A Catalyst

you honored your wife is emotionally filling in every way. Her demise was hideous and unscrupulous. I am personally disgusted and embarrassed, by the individuals who permit injustices such as the one that murdered your wife. Your stories will not be ignored. The 13th, 14th, and 15th Amendments should always be prominent. Because of them, everyone's life in the United States of America can thrive."

"Megan, your moral integrity has been felt by me. When you tell my story in the book, you are also telling my wife's story," President Lincoln stated. In the next moment, he stood and placed his hands together in prayer position, he bowed and said, "May peace be with you." He stood back up, turned, and exited the tent.

At this time Jesus stood up and bowed to me while saying, "Blessings received. You will help heal a great man by sharing his story." Jesus turned around and exited the tent.

Archangel Michael stood and asked, "Will you please follow Me? I have something I would like to show you."

I stood up and followed Archangel Michael out of the tent. We walked side by side for a few minutes to a lake with a magnificent waterfall as the backdrop. Sitting around a golden table waiting for us was Prophet Muhammad, Paramahansa Yogananda, King David, Kwan Yin, and Sitting Bull. At this time, I was instructed to sit between Prophet Muhammad and Archangel Michael. Prophet Muhammad began, "I wrote seventy-two percent of the Quran. It is stated on earth that I could not read or write. This is false. Reading and writing are what I enjoyed most. You must let this be known in your book that I received apparitions from God, Archangel Michael, and King David. King David did write Zabur, the psalms, and He also wrote the Torah. Moses wrote the Jewish commandments. All 613 were given to Him by God on Mt. Sinai. Moses also parted the Red Sea. Jesus wrote the Gospel in the old testament."

Paramahansa Yogananda said, "It was Sage Vyasa who wrote the Bhagavad Gita based upon the apparitions from Lord Krisna. Many believe there are multiple authors and know not when it was composed. It was written in the second century BC. The reason for Sage Vyasa's absence and my presenting the Bhagavad Gita information to you is because He chose to reincarnate many times."

Sitting Bull picked up the conversation, "I was a Hunkpapa Lakota holy man. I am to tell you the creation of all things learned by the Native Americans is derived from Christianity. Christianity is comprised of the ways of Christ. We love all things."

Kwan Yin began, "I am the embodiment of love and magic. Love is magic and magic is love. I was a Buddhist in My choice of faith. I followed His teachings of the Four Noble Truths and the Noble 8-Fold Path."

Archangel Michael said, "Each of these beautiful souls is going to read to your teachings from the Quran, the Torah, the Bhagavad Gita, the Old Testament, and the Buddhist canon consisting of the Sutras. You will not be tested as We know what is read to you will become live in your cell memory. Your cell memory also includes your soul memory. As you write about each of Us the necessary memory for what you will write will be available. Let us begin."

For what felt like hours I sat and listened to each of my instructors read to me and answer my questions. I understood everything like it was a natural way of being.

A Catalyst

When we were finished, Archangel Michael took me to violin class.

Violin class is a mandatory activity in Heaven. The violin and piano are the two instruments perfectly aligned with the chakras in everybody. A scientific code is expressed when the instrument is played in the 528 Hz range or higher. Mozart oversees writing music for the violin classes in Heaven.

There were what felt like thousands of students sitting in golden chairs with gold music stands before each chair. On the stand was sheet music that was played by us all. We sounded like an amazing orchestra.

I sat in the front row next to Archangel Michael. Playing violin was effortless for me. As it turns out, everyone can play effortlessly in Heaven. God and Goddess sat in huge golden chairs watching us as if They were at a concert. Their chairs were placed in front of three rows of golden bleachers. When we had finished playing our music, I heard a whoosh sound above me. I looked up and saw about thirty Archangels fly in to stand on the bleachers behind God and Goddess. When each Archangel was standing still Archangel Michael stood up and walked over to the bleachers to join Them. He stood right behind God and Goddess. The Archangels began to sing in Latin a most glorious sound. What They were singing reminded me of the choir I used to hear when I was a child in the Latin masses at church. The Archangels sang for about twenty minutes straight and it was beautiful. God closed His eyes throughout the entire performance. When the singing stopped, God stood up and reached for Goddess's hand. When She took Him, she stood and turned with God to face the Archangels. Both bowed to show Their thanks. The Archangels then flew away just as They had flown in. All of them except

Megan C Brown

Archangel Michael came back and took my hand. I turned and placed my violin and bow on the chair I sat in and walked with Archangel Michael to our next meeting place.

We walked in silence for a moment on the sidewalk next to beautiful grass. "You all sounded so beautiful Archangel Michael. I have never heard anything so beautiful in my life," I said.

"Blessings received," He said with a smile. "We have a surprise for you now. Are you ready for a concert of another kind?"

As I looked at Archangel Michael as He spoke to me, I did not notice the man approaching me from the side. Archangel Michael stopped and reached His arms out to hug Freddie Mercury. Freddie is a favorite singer of mine from a rock group called, 'Queen.' Freddie smiled at me and asked, "How are you doing?"

I responded politely, "I am in a lot of pain on earth right now. I am in kidney failure caused by a rare autoimmune disease TTP-HUS."

"Are you ready for a concert?" Freddie asked me.

"Yes," I responded immediately. I was so excited to hear him sing live. This was one of the surprises God told me I would be experiencing. The three of us walked up to the backstage area. Freddie went up the stairs on the side of the stage and waited to be introduced for his show. Archangel Michael and I went out to the audience and stood in the front row. There was an opening performance by Billy Barty, Spike Jones, and the City Slickers, and the Other Orchestra. They performed three songs and kept the audience laughing. When they finished, Bob Hope came out on stage and did some stand-up comedy as only he could do. When he finished, he introduced Ella Fitzgerald who came out and sang

A Catalyst

three songs. When Ella left the stage Bob Hope came back out and told some more jokes until he introduced Dizzy Gillespie. Dizzy played three songs and what a soul groove of sound he played. When he was done, out came Marvin Gaye. I remember Marvin singing 'I Heard It Through the Grapevine,' 'Sexual Healing,' and 'Ain't No Mountain High Enough.' It was awesome to hear all these performers while dancing with Archangel Michael, and some of the saints and ascended masters that greeted me in Synagogue after my life review. Yes, I even danced with Jesus.

When Marvin was finished Bob Hope went back out on stage while the next band was getting ready to perform. Then Mr. Hope announced Rick James. What a ball of energy. Rick jumped up, did the splits, and sang to the depths of his soul. After his three songs were finished, Mr. Hope came back out to the stage to tell a few more jokes while the next band got ready.

Finally, it was time for Freddie Mercury. The curtains opened and there stood Freddie wearing a white t-shirt with rolled-up sleeves and a pack of cigarettes in the left sleeve. Terry Kath was on bass. Rick James was on guitar. Marvin Gaye was on the piano. Buddy Rich was on drums. The second piano was for Freddie during the piano duals in 'Bohemian Rhapsody,' Play the Game,' and 'Love of My Life.' The band played about fifteen Queen songs and I was in Heaven literally and figuratively speaking. I danced in groups with Jesus, Archangel Michael, Kali, and Kwan Yin to name a few. I even slowed danced with Julius Caesar to 'Love of My Life.'

The concert ended after the last song 'Bohemian Rhapsody.' Archangel Michael took my right hand and Jesus took my left hand. Both were as filled with energy and excitement as I was after watching an incredible two-hour show. "Did you have fun, Megan?" Jesus asked.

"I have never been to a better show in my life," I replied with excitement.

"Did you ever think you would slow dance with Julius Caesar?" Archangel Michael questioned.

"Not in a million years, Archangel Michael. Not in a trillion years," I said.

"We are taking you to our next stop. Back to your tent," Jesus said.

"Am I going back to class now?" I asked Jesus.

"Not yet, love. There is more fun awaiting you," Archangel Michael replied.

"Well, I have to thank God for this experience. I guess thank you notes are out of the question," I announced.

Both Jesus and Archangel Michael laughed at my statement. "Archangel Michael answered, "You will have a chance to thank Him."

At this time, Jesus entered my tent followed by me and Archangel Michael. There was a large golden table with eight golden pitchers on it filled with red wine, and eight golden bread baskets filled with sourdough rolls. Seated at the table waiting for us were Ella Fitzgerald, Dizzy Gillespie, Billy Barty, Spike Jones, and the City Slickers and the Other Orchestra, Buddy Rich, Marvin Gaye, Rick James, Terry Kath, Bob Hope, and Freddie Mercury. Jesus pulled out a golden chair for me directly across from Freddie. Jesus sat to my immediate left, and Archangel Michael sat to my immediate right just like in Synagogue after my life review. Everyone welcomed us as we sat. Golden cherubs were fluttering around the table waiting to pour wine in our glasses as they got low. The cherubs hovered above us in the background while

A Catalyst

occasionally swooping in to refill the bread baskets. The Archangels never drank or ate anything.

There was lots of dialogue and laughter around the table. It was a fantastic feeling of joy for what seemed like for us all. After about an hour, we received a surprise visit. Hundreds of golden cherubs began filling the tent. In walked Prophet Muhammad. There were golden cherubs that lit up the outside of the entire tent. All of us sitting at the table were visibly taken by surprise. We stood instantly and bowed. Hundreds of golden Angels followed Prophet Muhammad into the tent. Three rows of Angels filled the entire interior of the tent. Many Angels were covering the entire exterior of the tent as well. The sky displayed the most unbelievable, bright white light, and golden rays I had ever seen.

All the Angels were radiating from within their golden shells, and their wings were a transparent gold. This was one of the most mind-blowing occurrences I have ever witnessed.

Prophet Muhammad ordered us to sit down. He continued to stand through His entire visit.

He began by looking directly at me, "You will let the world know of My existence. You will inform every one of My true desires. All false messages containing negativity must be eradicated. Your message to Islam must be extremely clear. I am Islam. I will continue to be involved throughout the Middle East. I have protected their lands throughout millenniums and will continue to do so. The bombing must stop. The senseless killings in the name of God are a lie. To justify slaughters in My name is irreparable. Conscious awareness of falsifications was administered pre-birth to the current Islam society. I witness faithfulness throughout today's Islam. Commendable. Islam must, to the root, obey My commands. I do not sway from God's desires. You will eradicate all pretenses. I am sending the most unconventional person to make known, worldwide, My desire. Not only will Islam adhere to My messages, so too, but will also the rest of the world. I tell you, young one, to blaze beyond one's comfort zone, in one's life. You will integrate every feeling of uncertainty breeding within one's mind, knowing truths are speaking throughout your cell memory. Listen to Me during questionable circumstances. I am always speaking to you and filling your entire being with endless love. I am more powerful than one comprehends from the earth. It will be known more rapidly My message to humanity, through more unconventional messages. One must break barriers currently suffocating one's mind. Mahdi is the highest frequency of love. Islam is considered a non-Christian religion. Let Me make it known to all, Prophet Muhammad and Jesus both delivered messages of love. Just as Jesus was the prophet to Israel, so too is Prophet Muhammad to the Middle East. To kill irresponsibly, like an Islam, is the same as a Christian killing an Islam, a Jew, a Serb, a Buddhist, a Hindu, a Native American, a Baha'i, a Sikh, or a Taoist. No one has a right to take lives, thriving with other lives. Those are rules left to God. This rule is never to be broken. Obtaining peace is Our mission. We will succeed using every avenue. The change will happen. Rewards are for those who adhere to the laws contained in your book."

I bowed my head and began to speak, "I have honored, Your Holiness, that You, Prophet Muhammad, have bestowed upon me Your faith. It is my mission to return to earth, and fulfill all orders instructed to me. Blessings received for Your unconditional love; you bestow for a nation who desperately needs it now. May I

A Catalyst

serve Your people with honesty and be received with the same love I intend to go back with. Blessings received."

When Prophet Muhammad spoke, I looked up. "My time allotted with you has come to an end here. Put the book out."

We quickly stood as Prophet Muhammad turned around to exit the tent. We bowed our heads. Prophet Muhammad exited just as He had arrived. Angels in the tent followed Him first, followed by the hundreds of Angels surrounding the exterior of the tent. The further away They got, the bluer the sky became.

We all looked at one another with a unanimous feeling of amazement. Each of us sat quietly for a moment, as we took everything in, we had just heard.

Marvin broke the silence with a uniformed seriousness. "I want you to write in your book, we realize what happened when we were children. I can only speak for some of us in here, including you Megan. It was because of Ella Fitzgerald, Dizzy Gillespie, Freddie Hubbard, Dr. Martin Luther King, Jr., and many others who faced injustices in humanity. Many people were spitting on, beaten, murdered, arrested, and humiliated because of skin color. This division was created by religion. Enforced for the wealthiest of those with bigger surpluses. Government officials declared people unlike themselves, those with darker skin, those who were not allowed in their churches because of skin color, expendable."

Freddie reminded everyone, "You forgot to mention sexual freedom. I was considered expendable too. The barbs, name-calling, and humiliation I endured for loving men weren't fun by any means."

Megan C Brown

As we were sitting and talking, I asked a question. "If you were allowed to say one more thing to the world, what would it be?"

Freddie started immediately with a stage-like presence. He sat up higher in his chair and threw up his right arm. "To all my friends and fans, no party, or performance I ever gave is as splendid, and sublime as the ongoing rituals enveloping my soul on this plateau. Freedom is boundless with no hitches on any level. I am still gay and loving every moment."

Slowly he sat back and took a drag of his cigarette. His eyes welled up with tears, and clearly, a new feeling came over him. After a pause, he said, "To the man who loved me to the other side, I still love you deeper in my soul than I knew how to tap into on earth. May knowing this be healing for you."

Then Freddie sat back and cried for a moment. Rick quickly got out of his chair and knelt next to Freddie while hugging him. I leaned over the table and extended both of my hands to him. Freddie leaned toward me and took my hands in his. All of us continued to quietly watch Freddie with love. When Freddie was ready to speak again, he said, "To my fans, I would say the energy coming through me, I was in touch with on every level. My entire being vibrated love while I performed on stages. The opening of my soul was magical, to say the least. It was out of my control as to the power of God, and His brilliance was unknown during my life as a human. My ego allowed me to think it was my talent only, with the courage to light up each performance. I believed that very well. I wasn't pompous, or shallow because I knew there existed something grander, to be sure. Listen to the songs, and what came through me, and us as a band. I would write a song for all of you, to catapult your

A Catalyst

knowledge, and save you from the destruction of humanity, currently all-encompassing because judgment determines most decisions. This crippling mind disease continues to destroy the consciousness of humanity. Come to your senses. All of them. Get in touch with your spiritual senses. You'll feel so much better, and realize we are on the same trip. Same trip, different experiences. In spades of course darling. I am still singing because a passion never dies. Its gloriousness is superlative to any dream one could ever have."

My heart was so touched by what I had just experienced, I felt I had to speak, "In my own life experiences, I know pain. The disgust I have felt when I encountered tormenting. I want all of you to know, I am raising my son to love everyone and their differences. I will continue to enforce upon him injustice is not tolerable. I know I have the power as his mother, to impart this way of coexisting."

"We know you will," said Marvin.

"You have the chance to go back and make a difference. You have seen the reality of the universe and get to go back as an adult without incarnating. We must incarnate and stumble through growing up again. We are counting on you, to say the things no one said for us with darker skin than yours. Make it known to everyone, we are all equal," proclaimed Rick.

I responded quickly, "I promise you all, I will write the book. I will share these conversations. I will tell everyone your truths."

"You tell every gay man and woman darling; we are perfect. We are not turned away from Heaven. We enhance it!" Freddie said with excitement as he threw his hands up in the air.

Megan C Brown

Throughout my entire experience with these men, the only time Buddy said a word was when everyone said, 'Yes.' Buddy's unspoken agreements were felt by us all.

What happened next was awe-inspiring to me. In walked Julius Caesar with golden cherubs following Him. Everyone at the table stood up once again, but Caesar used His hands motioning us to sit down. A beautiful golden chair was brought in by, Archangel Raphael and Archangel Gabriel, for Caesar to sit in. He did. He sat directly to my left at the head of the table. Both Archangels stood to Caesar's left and right side. Then, Caesar spoke in His beautiful Italian accent, "I have come here by God's orders to gift you with My story that includes the magnificence of forgiveness and faith. I will share with you in this now a piece of My beautiful love story of Cleopatra and me. We met at a celebration I was giving for peace in My palace. I was the new ruler of the Roman Empire. I had many visions of the order being had for all. I quickly incorporated the coming together of Eastern and Western Europe for peace talks to be made for us all. You know this as being the United Nations. Your history books have made My history on earth very different than what has happened. Marc Antony and I were friends. He was someone I trusted completely. He was My, how shall I say? He was My right-hand man. Does this make sense to you, Megan?"

"Yes. Absolutely," I said confidently.

"I trusted him with My life. We worked together toward peace for many years. We agreed on everything. There was no stronger force of government to have existed at that time. I could dictate with ease because I had built up the trust of those around Me and in surrounding countries. There was one who ruled as I did.

A Catalyst

Cleopatra. Her instincts were superb, and so too was her way with the people. I met Cleopatra in My domain on this one evening. She was a force of absolute strength I had never felt before. I watched her walk into the party surrounded by her protection of people. I never saw anyone own a room like that before. I had never set eyes upon anyone as beautiful as her in My life. I was forty years old at the time and had never been married. I immediately walked up to her and introduced Myself. It was love at first sight for Me. I was with her throughout the entire evening. I even asked her to sit with Me for dinner and the dancing entertainment afterward. We were with one another for three full days. We never left one another. When she did leave Me to return to her country, I was beside Myself. I was never more changed by a person in My entire life. She was all I could think about. I had to make her My wife. I made plans to travel to her country immediately. Within days I was traveling to be by her side permanently. As it turned out, she could not stop thinking about Me either. We were married in Egypt in her home. Within the coming year, Cleopatra gave up the throne to her brother Ptolemy XIV. She reigned with Me in Western Europe until our sudden deaths after I won the vote of the people to stay as ruler in the Roman Empire. What matters most is our love for one another. She fulfilled Me in every way. There was nothing more important than our family unit. When we had Augustus, I felt I had everything. She was My best friend, a wonderful mother, and the only love of My life. Why am I telling you this story no one knows about? I want to impart with you the necessity of love. Until I met Cleopatra, I was amiss of something, but did not know. I had no desire to have brought to Me a woman to be My wife. A few very noble statesmen tried to introduce Me to

Megan C Brown

their daughters, but I rejected the notion immediately. I became known as the forever bachelor. I was untouchable. I was untouchable until love's powerful energy touched Me. Made Me wake up to a new way of being. She was My match. My soulmate. I learned to regard love with great respect. Nothing had ever made Me want to change My ways. I did not know it was possible to feel internally a longing for one person. I have felt it. Love is important to be worthy of attention. There was nothing more gratifying to Me than knowing we needed one another for strength. I became weak at the knees as you say on earth. I did anything for My wife, and she did anything to make Me feel loved. How is this story I come to you with connected with forgiveness and faith? It happens in life that truth becomes different. This is what happened with Marc Antony, Octavia, Cleopatra, and Myself. Marc Antony was never married to My wife, Cleopatra. He could not have been because he was already married to Octavia, his one and only spouse. We were not permitted multiple wives according to our religious beliefs. We were all practicing conservative Jews. The excessive number of Greek Gods and Goddesses are an inherent part of history due to the Greeks taking over the Roman Empire for a short period. They murdered My wife and me on the same night. Marc Antony could not have ruled because he and his wife were murdered on the same night as well. Marc Antony has been made into a rival of mine. We were never rivalling, only friends. When We all met here in Heaven after our deaths, we were aware of history having been damaged. It affected each of us differently, but our common denominator was sadness that humanity could never know the truth of what happened. Over time Cleopatra incarnated as did Octavia. Marc Antony and I

A Catalyst

have stayed friends, but because of the major life changes of being in Heaven, we have not spoken of those days since shortly after We arrived here. I have had to learn to forgive those that took our lives on earth and rewrote history. This forgiveness was and is personal. I have learned to hold on to the greatest love story of that time on earth. Me and Cleopatra. The story of Cleopatra and I may have been rewritten by others to change the course of history, but a soul connection can never be changed. A soul is an immaterial part of a being regarded as immortal. The soul is everlasting energy. The everlasting energy is loves purest form assigned to give life. As you can see love's purest forms are in Heaven as well. We are no longer human here. We are only everlasting energy. As you see Me in this now, I am love dressed in a human body surrounding my eternal energy of love.

Forgiveness was necessary for me to learn during my moments. I was being portrayed as a tyrant, having multiple marriages, a divorce, three children, and no marriage to Cleopatra. I felt I was being punished in Heaven. How is this possible I wondered? I was being portrayed on earth as someone I never was. Now I am in Heaven. Who am I, Megan? Am I earth's version of Gaius Julius Caesar, or Heaven's version? I am both. I have transitioned from one planet to another. My history book of self is My soul. My soul self can never be changed. Every moment I have lived is engraved in the Akashic records. These records are a matrix of being containing every creation in the galactic library that is love's energy source.

There is nothing I can do to change history on earth from Heaven. What I learned to make a difference was how I think about everything. I know what the truth is, and this is all that matters. It must be this way. If I should

213

rely on others for validation of My Life with Cleopatra, then I am missing the point. It is not another soul to have felt the oneness Cleopatra and I had. It is My soul. Our history exists as an engraving in the Akashic records. This book of galactic records will never be rewritten.

Please never forget what I am going to share with you in this now. 1 Corinthians 13, 'If I shall speak with every human and Angelic language and have no love in me, I shall be clanging brass or a noise-making cymbal. And if I have prophecy, and I know all mysteries and all knowledge and if I have all faith so that I may remove mountains, and I have no love in me, I would be nothing. And if I should feed everything that I have to the poor, and if I hand over my body to be burned up and I have no love in me, I gain nothing. Love is patient and sweet; love does not envy; love is not upset either puffed up. Love does not commit what is shameful, neither does it seek its own; it is not provoked, neither does it entertain evil thoughts, Rejoices not in evil, but rejoices in the truth, Endures all things, believes all things, hopes all, bears all. Love never fails; for prophecies shall cease, tongues shall be silenced, and knowledge will be nothing; For we know partially and we prophesy partially, But when perfection shall come, then that which is partial shall be nothing. When I was a child, I was speaking as a child, I was led as a child, I was thinking as a child, but when I became a man, I ceased childish things. Now we see as in a mirror, in an allegory, but then face-to-face. Now I know partially, but then I shall know as I am known. For there are these three things that endure: Faith, Hope, and Love, but the greatest of these is Love.'

It is with this Bible quote I stay close to My soul purpose. It was God who quoted it to Me when I approached Him for His guidance shortly after I arrived

A Catalyst

in Heaven. I have great satisfaction now knowing what I have done as a leader of the Roman Empire and as Cleopatra's husband was with love. With passion I served Rome. With passion, I served My wife Cleopatra and our son Augustus. What I have come to believe is there are two lives I have been forced to accept. My life on earth and My life in Heaven. Both are tied to My soul. I must answer to Myself in addition to God. Both of Us are watching My actions to serve love. It is My thoughts I can control and no one else. It is God who gave each of us the power to choose. This was His gift to every soul. I must choose to serve love. It is the most powerful energy. My love for Rome can never change earth's history books, but it can revolutionize how I speak to you in this now. My love for Cleopatra will also never change earth's history books, but she will live in My soul memory eternally as the one love I honored in My life on earth. What is greater? Proving a point, or knowing? Knowing who I am is the key to My eternal happiness. Knowing within Myself I have completed energy in My life course that is true to Me. What this means is every feeling I have about serving Rome was done with integrity. Every feeling I have about My wife Cleopatra is filled with loyalty, admiration, and love. What I have discovered is the secret to happiness lies within Me. I am cleared in My mind of any doubts and discrepancies surrounding My earth life and My life in Heaven. There is a difference between you and everyone else who will read our conversation. All of you only know what is written on earth. What I am sharing with you is much bigger than My earth story. I am starting with you a conversation to introduce to you the possibility of change must first happen within you for you to achieve clarity on a personal level. Your mind must choose to accept the truth no matter how it sounds.

Megan C Brown

Truth is that which is following fact and reality. Here in Heaven facts are shown in life reviews. I will share with you a portion of Mine when we meet with God again later so your mind has proof. The evidence you need will provide you with the absolute knowledge that what I say to you is accurate. You will return to earth and convey My messages in your book without hesitation. It will be others' opinions of what you will have written to make you pause. A temporary stop in your actions will occur, but you will continue because truth and cause for love to be understood are paramount in your soul mission. You will never let any of us down with what you bring to light on the pages of your book. All we ask is that you share your truth of this experience here in Heaven," Caesar stated.

He sat and looked at me, as did everyone else at the table and the Angels hovering around the tent. I can only imagine everyone must have been wondering what I was thinking. I felt a huge responsibility was being placed on me by, incredible thinkers and activists in our earth's history. Each meeting with me was by God's orders to bring about a personal understanding so that I may go back and present it to every individual who reads my story. The relief Caesar had just gifted me with was the same as what Goddess had gifted me with shortly after my life review in Synagogue. It was not my responsibility to make people believe the stories. It was only my duty to write them and publish them.

"Caesar, may I ask You a question?" I asked sincerely.

"Please do so," Caesar replied.

"It is my belief true feelings of love can never be felt by anyone outside of the relationship. Will You promise

A Catalyst

me You will never be disappointed with how I convey Your love story with Cleopatra?" I asked.

"Never will I be disappointed by you, Megan. You are My cause to make happen the truth I have always wanted to make known. I say to you blessings received for your bravery and reverence to God. Without it, none of us would be able to help love be perceived," Caesar said softly.

"When I come back to Heaven, Caesar, will You meet with me again to let me know how You feel?" I asked.

"Absolutely," Caesar said with a smile.

"Blessings received," I answered politely.

"There is one more thing I want you to write about: my son, Augustus. He was the creation of love by Cleopatra and me. He was cherished by Us. I want to say blessings received to Marc Antony's son Ptolemy Philadelphus who took My son to safety. Without him, my son Augustus would never have ruled. He was four years of age when his mother and I were murdered. He has incarnated as a very powerful political figure. I am extremely proud of him," Caesar ended.

"Caesar, please forgive my boldness," I said softly.

"I like bold, Megan," Caesar replied with a smile.

"Okay," I said, "Who is Your son?"

"I cannot tell you. Besides, no one would believe it, including My son," Caesar responded. "Someday he will come home to Me and we will have much to share."

"I had to ask Caesar," I said.

"I know. I'm glad you did. This is one of the truths you will write about with faith and trust," Caesar replied softly.

"I will Caesar," I replied respectfully.

Megan C Brown

"It is time for us to meet with God and watch pieces of My life review as Julius Caesar. Please come with Me," Caesar said softly. Caesar stood up and reached out His right hand to take my left hand. Both Archangel Raphael and Archangel Gabriel removed the golden chair that Caesar sat in. He held my hand and we exited the tent. This time Archangel Michael did not come with us, but I do not know why.

As Caesar and I entered Synagogue, God was seated in His chair at the head of His golden table. No one else was with Him this time. "Welcome," announced God. "Please be seated." God pointed for Caesar to sit directly next to Him where Jesus sat during my first visit after my life review, and He pointed to the chair directly to the right of Caesar for me to sit in where I sat during my first visit. "How did you like your meeting with Caesar?"

"Oh God, it was so beautiful. Blessings received," I said softly.

"What do you think of His love story," God asked me.

"It is unlike anything anyone on earth knows at this time. I am deeply honored to write about Caesar's truth," I replied.

"What do you think Caesar's faith is about?" God questioned.

"His faith that love will ultimately prevail?" I answered with a question.

"Do you want to answer My question with a question?" God asked me with a serious tone.

The truth is I did not know what to say. So, I got really honest with God. "God I am so nervous right now. I don't know what to say. I didn't know Psalm 91. I didn't know 1 Corinthians 13. I don't know the power of Prophet Prophet Muhammad on earth. I had no idea

218

A Catalyst

Caesar and Cleopatra even existed. God, I am guilty of not believing in much before I got here to Heaven. Why You want me to write this book for You is still mind-boggling to me. I feel like I have already failed You and I haven't even gotten back to earth yet. Please forgive me. I realize I can only be honest with You. So here I am sounding like I don't know what. I am so sorry. I don't know what else to say," I replied respectfully.

"You are a perfectionist I see before Me. What do you think of yourself?" God asked.

"Well God, now I'm going to piss You off. I don't feel too great about myself. I'm still holding on to past stuff. I don't know how to forgive, and I haven't forgotten many things that have happened to me. Here I am sitting before my Creator feeling like I am insulting You. I want to learn to forgive God. I want to get on with my life and not let my past dictate my future. Please I am begging You. Will You help me?" I quietly responded.

God began, "I love your honesty, Megan. I find it to be quite refreshing. You'd be surprised what I hear in Heaven. Men, women, and children still try to lie. They eventually get over their old habits. So, I want you to hear that I am paying you a compliment. Blessings received for sharing with Me your fears. You are safe with Me. Will you trust Me in this now to be your guide?"

At this moment I felt tears of embarrassment and relief well up and roll down my cheeks. I answered God with the greatest respect," I would be honored, Your Holiness."

"Good. Let us get started. Caesar, did You love Your wife Cleopatra?" God asked.

"With all of My heart," Caesar responded.

"How did it make You feel to know all of the earth was being lied to about You Caesar?" God questioned.

Megan C Brown

"Angry at first," Caesar replied.

"How do You feel about Cleopatra in this now?" God asked Caesar.

"I am still as in love with her now as I was then," Caesar said softly.

"Why," God asked.

"Because love never dies," Caesar said.

"That is so. What else do You feel Caesar?" God asked.

"Now I feel relief God," Caesar replied.

"Why?" God questioned.

"Because I know who I am. I know My love for Cleopatra was real. I did not love her to acquire anyone's approval. Therefore, I did not die with My wife to acquire anyone's approval either. I was happy knowing we died together, and I was by her side. It was she who brought Me the greatest joy I had ever known in My life," Caesar responded respectfully.

"What is this joy You speak of Caesar," God asked.

"It is My internal degree and amount of love I had never equated with another soul God. Nothing I had ever experienced before Cleopatra walked into My life had a measure," Caesar replied.

"How beautiful Caesar. Please tell Megan what You meant about faith," God ordered.

"I had a strong belief in You God. After We spoke one time about how some of the doctrines of Judaism were based upon spiritual apprehension, I realized I was sitting before You. You are My proof," Caesar said.

"That is so. Megan, I am every faith serving peace. What is peace you wonder? Peace is simply freedom from war and violence. Religion has caused multiple wars and violence. So, what am I talking about? It goes back to what each of Us said to you here at My table after your life

220

A Catalyst

review. Acceptance is synonymous with love. This is the key to unlock every door to peace by way of religion. Do you understand what I am saying, Megan?" God asked.

"I understand You want me to help spread a message on earth about love. This is something that sounds so beautiful, but this message I have never heard before on earth," I responded.

"Indeed, it is a beautiful message. You will help Me and Caesar and all of Us here in Heaven. We need you to help create a passageway for everyone on earth who reads this book I have ordered you to write. A way for the believers in Me and non-believers in Me to come together by way of Me. When everyone is validated by way of God who was created by way of science, it becomes a union of not only the minds and every soul connected to the individual's mind but of humanity. Love is humanity's equalizer," God said.

Caesar began, "Megan, I am Rome's previous ruler. Who am I here in Heaven? Am I a ruler of Rome now? No. I am a descendant of God serving as love's prolific group in Heaven. I need you to go back and tell the world love rules all. In the end when one makes it into Heaven, one will learn what We are saying to be true."

"Why are you being asked to transport this knowledge you have inquired? Why not? You have stated you believed in nothing before you got here. What do you believe in this now?" God asked me.

I began to well up with tears again. This time I felt like I owed God and Caesar apologies for having told Them I didn't believe in Them. I never thought They were trying to make me feel bad or guilty for my having shared my truth with Them. It was quite the opposite They made me notice. I only received a feeling of love from both. So, when I decided it was time for an apology, it was me who needed to remove the uncomfortable feeling I had placed on myself at God's table. "I feel the need to tell You both how sorry I am for not having believed in either of You. Now I feel qualified to answer Your question, God. I believe in You, God, the Father, the Almighty, Creator of Heaven and earth; and in Jesus Christ, Your

"Megan, there is the ending of innocence, the ending of a life, the ending of a marriage, the ending of a belief. With every end is a new beginning. You are ending a way of life as you once knew it. Do you agree?" God asked me. Son; Who was conceived by Holy Spirit, born of the Virgin Mary; suffered under Pontius Pilate, was crucified, died, and was buried. He descended into hell; the third day He rose again from the dead; He ascended into Heaven, is seated at the right hand of You, God the Father Almighty; from thence He shall come to judge the living and the dead. I believe in the Holy Spirit, the Holy Catholic Church, the communion of saints, the forgiveness of sins, the resurrection of the body, and life everlasting. Amen."[1]

"You remembered the Apostles Creed. How do you feel in this now?" God asked.

"I feel amazing. Maybe Caesar's meeting with me did something wonderful to my memory. Blessings received, Caesar," I said directly to Caesar with a smile.

"You are so welcome, Megan," Caesar responded gently with a smile.

"God, if I may I'd like to share my favorite prayer with You," I announced politely.

"Please do so," God replied with a smile.

---

[1] Felix, Richard. The Apostles' Creed. Pilot Grove, Mo: Our Faith Press, 1935. Print.

A Catalyst

While I looked into God's eyes, I began speaking, "Our Father, who art in Heaven. Hallowed be Thy name. Thy kingdom come, thy will be done, on earth as it is in Heaven. Give us this day our daily bread, and forgive us our trespasses as we forgive those who trespass against us. And lead us not into temptation, but deliver us from evil. For thine is the kingdom, the power, and the glory, forever and ever. Amen."

"Why is this your favorite prayer, Megan?" God asked.

"Because I understand it now, You are in Heaven. You are honored. The kingdom of Heaven has come for me, but I must go back and do on earth for You here in Heaven. I am asking You to continue feeding me so that I may serve You. I am asking You to forgive me for everything I have done. I am asking You to help me to learn forgiveness. I do not want to be led into temptation away from You. Please protect me from evil. Heaven is Your kingdom, the power, and the glory, forever and ever. I believe," I answered softly.

"Are you forever changed, Megan?" Caesar asked.

"Yes, Caesar. Honestly, I do not want to go back, but I know that I have to. You are ordering me to go back to God. I hope I don't have to stay long," I responded.

"You will be back, but I cannot tell you when," God replied.

"I understand. That would not be fair to anyone else," I said.

"That is so," God said softly.

"I would like to know when you are coming back so we may speak some more, but God will not tell me either," Caesar quipped.

"Not even You?" I joked aloud, "Well, God, come on. Don't You ever want to tell anyone?"

Megan C Brown

"I made a vow to Holy Spirit that I will never release love's ending date written in the timeline to anyone," God informed me.

"Isn't that a lot of pressure on You?" I asked God.

"Not at all. It is how love programmed Me," God answered.

"God, do I ask You too many questions?" I wondered.

"Not at all. You may ask Me anything You like," God answered.

"Have You been married to Goddess since love's creation of You? Did Holy Spirit create Goddess for You, or did You create Goddess for You?" I asked.

"You are curious. This is beautiful to witness. Holy Spirit created Goddess at My request so that I would not be alone," God answered.

"Please keep asking, Megan," Caesar joked, "I haven't heard any of this." We all laughed.

"You pulled a woman from earth who needs to see it to believe it. Now that I've seen both of You, you can tell me anything and I'll believe it," I said with a sincere laugh. "Now I want to know about Jesus." We all laughed at my comment.

"Ask Me anything," God said.

"I would love to know if You have meetings with one another," I inquired.

"About what?" God asked.

"Don't You have to converse about the amount of love a soul created in his or her lifetime?" I wondered.

"I already know," God said with ease.

"That's right. You're God. Forgive me please because a light bulb just got turned on in my thought process," I joked.

A Catalyst

Caesar chimed in, "I love watching this conversation. I never get to see anyone ask God questions like this. Keep going, Megan."

"I want You both to know I am asking my questions with absolute respect," I said.

"We are not offended Megan," God replied, "Please continue if you like."

"How long do people stay in Heaven?" I asked.

"As long as they need to before they reincarnate," God informed me.

"A recycled soul?" I questioned.

"Yes. With all the information of every previous life included in the next life," God informed me.

"I'm not trying to be funny God, but is this why everyone is so confused?" I asked.

"What is this confusion you speak of?" God asked.

"Well, if I may use religion as my example, I would have to ask why a lack of understanding of love exists throughout the world," I announced.

"Beautiful question, Megan," Caesar said.

"It is quite beautiful indeed. The recipe for love has never been written before. Without the ingredients how is creation possible?" God asked.

"Nothing can be created without the directions," I answered.

"That is so. We have given you the ingredients. Now you can write the recipe for Us," God stated.

"I will God. I promise," I said, "There are so many other questions I have, but they are not about love."

"What are they about?" God asked.

"Why have I faced so much pain in my life, God?" I asked.

"There are different ways by which a soul will learn Megan. You have already stated you must see to believe.

Megan C Brown

You have experienced a life filled with beginnings and endings. Would you agree?" God questioned.

"Yes," I replied.

"You have been witness to answers in your life. Your answers came to you in the form of endings. Endings are to teach you how to let go. Nothing is constant but change."

"God, do You mean my health is now compromised because of kidney failure?" I asked.

"That is only a small piece. You now believe in love. You now believe in Me. You believe in Caesar. You believe in Prophet Muhammad. You believe in Jesus. You believe in Heaven. How do you think all of this translates to you on earth?" God asked.

"I don't know God," I said softly.

"How can you know until you live your life?" God questioned.

"I guess I can't know," I replied.

"No, you cannot. There are so many elements to life. You must interact with others. You have your choices and others have their choices. A domino effect begins not only emotionally, spiritually, and physically, but privately, in marriages, friendships, communities, cities, states, countries, and globally. Do you think you will create a domino effect in your life and the lives of others when you go back?" God asked.

"I will find out when I go back," I said.

"That is so," God stated.

"Are you ready to go back?" Caesar asked.

"Do I have a choice as to when I go back?" I asked Caesar.

"No sweetheart. You do not," Caesar replied kindly.

"I guess I'm as ready as I'll ever be," I said.

"That is so," God said.

226

A Catalyst

"Are You sending me back now, God?" I asked.

"Not yet. I have something else very special planned for you. We are leaving in this now to join Archangel Michael, Archangel Ezra, Archangel Gabriel, Archangel Raphael, Archangel Nathaniel, Archangel Ariel, Archangel Chamuel, Archangel Raziel, all of the Archangels, Jesus, Prophet Muhammad, Sitting Bull, Goddess, Mahatma Gandhi, Kali, Paramahansa Yogananda, White Eagle, King David, Buddha, and everyone who greeted you in Synagogue after your life review," God announced.

"Please take My hand," Caesar said as He stood up and reached out His left hand for mine, "I want you to know you are not alone."

"Blessings received," I said to Caesar as I took His hand. At this moment I felt honored to be holding the hand of the once Roman Emperor. More than this though I felt extremely comforted by a man who made Himself equal to me when He explained how He serves love. Julius Caesar had an incredible force of strength I could feel. He carried Himself with integrity and kindness.

God was ahead of Caesar and me the entire walk. It took about ten minutes to get to a hill where I saw God and Goddess' white house on the top. There were gardens around it with vibrant colored flowers and beautiful green grass. Across the yard down a hill was a giant golden table in front of the beautiful lake and waterfall. God led us to the table. As we got closer, I could see everyone seated around the table. I had seen them all in Synagogue after my life review. Jesus, Archangel Michael, El Morya, Mary, and St. Germain were the only ones standing up as We approached the table. As Caesar took me to my chair between Jesus and Archangel Michael, God sat at the head of His table. Caesar

227

announced, "This is Megan's last visit with all of Us at this table. It is in this now We will stand and hold hands to commemorate her visit. Let us bow our heads and pray. God, Jesus, Archangel Michael, Mary, El Morya, St. Germain, and everyone at this table I ask that You stay close to Megan in her coming days, months, and years. Please inspire her with Your words of wisdom, gentility, and love. May each of Us continue to work Our magic to assist Megan from Heaven as she finishes her journey on earth. We look to you sweetheart to begin spreading the word of love on earth. When you wonder why you have lived, we will always remind you about the book. It will take you a while, but your ways of being will be refined in those times. You will succeed. We have no doubts." Caesar pulled the chair out for me to sit down in and then walked around to His chair that was to the left of Mary.

God announced, "Please be seated. Megan, it was ordered of Me by Holy Spirit to give you a proper sending-off party. We all know how much you love the music by Queen. I have asked Freddie Mercury to come up with a show of his creation. Before We watch the much-anticipated performances, I have asked Freddie to come and sit with all of Us here at the table and tell Us what his favorite song is and why."

God raised His right hand and looked over my shoulder. Standing to my right was Freddie Mercury. I stood up and we hugged one another. After our hug, Freddie sat to my immediate right and the left of Archangel Michael.

Freddie began, "I am honored to have been asked by You God to perform for love. My favorite song is 'Barcelona.' When I wrote it with another gentleman, I could feel the love of God come through me. The words were effortless and the excitement to sing it with a most

A Catalyst

beautiful soul lifted me from within. Her voice was golden. Long live her voice in my soul. It still echoes in my soul as I harken back to the first time, we performed it together. She gave me one of the greatest thrills I had ever received in my life."

God asked, "Megan, how long have you been listening to Queen?"

"Since I was eleven years old. I remember hearing 'Another One Bites the Dust.' Freddie, your voice was so commanding and convincing. I had never heard anyone like you before," I said.

God said, "I have asked Freddie to sit next to you and join all of Us for a going-away celebration. Before the show starts, does Anyone have anything They would like to say?"

At this time Kali stood up and said, "When you need to talk to someone, please talk to Me. I will listen to you without judgment. I wish I could walk this walk with you in human form, but I will walk with you in Angel form instead."

Kali was so sweet. I looked over at God and asked, "God can I give Kali a hug?"

"Yes," God replied with a smile.

I walked around the table behind God to the chair straight across from me. Kali turned and put Her arms out and I walked right into them and hugged Her with my head on Her shoulder. We hugged for a minute, and I pulled away, respectfully kissed Her on Her cheek, and walked back to my chair.

Prophet Muhammad said, "Megan you are a blessing in disguise. I am so happy We have had the opportunity to sit and converse in a relaxed atmosphere here in Heaven. May you go back with your armor in

Megan C Brown

place for the walk of a lifetime. We will be with you. I will always be at your side."

"Blessings received," I responded.

God announced while pointing behind me, "It is time for a show. Let Us in this now place Our attention on Bob Hope."

At this time there was a stage behind me, and Bob Hope was indeed standing center stage. He began looking right at me, "Did you ever wonder why? Why are you in Heaven with all of Us? Yeah, I've been wondering the same thing." Laughter was heard around the entire table.

After about half an hour of laughs with Bob Hope, Jack Benny performed. His opening, "Were you planning on staying? That's funny God. I don't remember her name being called for the lineup of this show."

God piped up, "She is the show!"

Jack said, "Oh, I'm sorry, God. I misunderstood You. Was that her life review I just watched?" To which everyone began to laugh because no one other than the person it is about and their guides watch another soul's life review.

When Jack was finished with his act, Henny Youngman took center stage. "Kidney failure? I thought she said boob knee failure. This would explain her saggy breasts and a bad knee. One body part compensating for another part." Everyone was laughing and some were clapping at what I thought was his cleverness.

Next on the list was Chris Farley. I missed his days on television because he was too late for me. Thankfully, God knew I have a bent sense of humor. These guys all played with it. Chris made himself known loud and clear. He spoke directly to me. "You're back! I didn't know you had left. So, when God told me he was having a soiree for

230

A Catalyst

you I laughed. I thought, come on God. Why would you go out of your way to make a person in Heaven feel all warm and fuzzy? What does she have the rest of us don't?" Then God laid it down for me. He said, 'Kidney failure.' I asked God, 'When was kidney failure allowed in Heaven?' God said, 'A few days ago.' Ba bam.

When Chris was finished, he left the stage. It was quiet for a moment. Then peeking out from the curtain on the side of the stage was a face who smiled directly at me. I knew I was in for it now. It was Richard Pryor. He came sauntering out on stage while laughing at me. He was saying, "Megan, Megan, oh sweet Megan. It's all downhill from here. The roast is on and I'm feeling a little dry. Let us moisten our lips, shall we?" At this point, Richard began whistling the opening of the Andy Griffith show. When he finished the song, he asked me to join him on stage. So, I did. He put his left arm around my neck and whispered out loud, 'Do you want to stay?'

"Yes," I said affirmatively.

"Wouldn't that be nice? You, me, and God hangin' out tellin' jokes. Who's gonna believe it? Everybody knows that line about God's wrath. Coming down off the mountain top holding a bolt of lightning in His left hand. Wielding it like a sword and shaking it back and forth. Now, what do you think He was thinking?" Richard asked me.

"I don't know this story either. Is this another Bible story?" I asked God in a playful voice. Everyone started laughing at the table.

"Yes," God replied.

"God, I failed again," I said. "Oh shit. I have to read it don't I to keep up with all of You?" Everyone including Richard Pryor was laughing hysterically, slapping their knees, clapping their hands, and whistling.

Megan C Brown

Richard said, "Oh girl, even I read the Bible! How do you think I got in this place? Who let you in? God. Did You know You let in a stray?"

"I'm afraid so, Richard. I have My ways," God replied.

"Damn. She must be something good," Richard stated. He picked up his left hand and began to count with his fingers, "She never read the Bible. Sex before marriage. Am I right, Megan?"

"Yes," I said with a smile on my face as I stood frozen not knowing what was going to come out of anyone's mouth.

"Look, she's smiles, God. Smiling about sex before marriage. Isn't that breaking some Catholic law?" Richard asked God.

"Yes," God said while He was smiling.

"Oh shit. I'm doomed now," I replied softly.

"Oh shit is right," Richard said.

"God, are You going to forgive me for having sex out of wedlock?" I asked.

"I already have," God shouted.

"Oh, Richard, I'm good now," I informed him.

"Will you look at that happy smile on your face? She's singing in the rain. Love is raining down on you sweetheart," Richard announced.

"I am eternally grateful," I said.

"Well, you better be!" Richard responded and everyone started laughing again.

As much fun as we were having there was still more to be had. When Richard finished after his hour-long stint, it was time for music. The music began with Johan Sebastian Bach playing an interlude for what was to come. The curtains on the stage stayed closed for a few moments and opened to a rainbow of colors on the

232

A Catalyst

clothing of the orchestra, and a beautiful woman wearing a floor-length red dress waiting for Freddie Mercury. Suddenly, the opening of 'Barcelona' began playing and Freddie got up and headed for the stage. He walked up on stage and into the center where he joined her. They began to sing, and it was beautiful. When this song was over, they sang one final song, 'You Take My Breath Away.' After the opening of the song God came around and stood before me. He reached out His left hand and I took it. He pulled me up and the two of Us danced the waltz as everyone watched.

When the song was finished God walked me over to my chair and I sat down. God walked back to His chair, and Freddie came back and sat at the table next to me. God did not sit down. He said, "I would like everyone to stand and pray with Me." Everyone at the table stood and held hands at this time. God began, "I wish for you the grace I have bestowed upon you to be felt by you and every soul you touch in the book. May your faith in Me never waiver. May Jesus be a part of your prayers. May Archangel Michael be a part of your prayers. May Every soul at My table be a part of your prayers. May Holy Spirit hear My prayer in this now. I wish for you enlightenment of an Angelic kind to wash you throughout your entire being in this now." At this moment when God said in this now, a white light lit up my body as I stood at His table. "As I bequeath you with My love, I ask you to honor Me from this moment forward. In My name, amen." God took a moment and looked around the table. He looked at me last and said, "Please be seated," and Everyone sat down.

After a moment, Jesus stood up and looked to His right at me seated next to Him. "I want you to remember Me, Megan. I am always at your side. Please call on Me in times of trouble and in times of thanks. In times of joy may you remember love as being your guiding force from Heaven. It is I who rejoices at your spiritual growth in this fortuitous visit. May your reigning guides be honored by, you, on earth from this moment forward. We love you." Jesus sat back down.

Archangel Michael stood and looked to His left to where I was seated. "I am honored to have been given these anticipated days with you. May you remember Me always in all ways. I am at your every beck and call. Please remember My patience with you. You will need this for your book. It is designed by Holy Spirit that We are here with you in this now. There are no mistakes, Megan. We are all here to help you reestablish your relationship with Us. It has begun again by this force you call kidney failure. We call it Divine timing. There is no mistake you are in great physical pain. It is to help you disconnect from the earth more easily to hear, learn, feel, and rejoice in love. The very essence you are to Us. There will come a time when the world will understand love. Blessings received for your service." Archangel Michael sat back down.

Across the table was Caesar. He stood and looked straight at me with His piercing blue eyes. "You are always welcome to call on Me when you pray. I will be attuned to you from this contact forward. I am not whom your history books say I am. I am much more. I serve God just as you do now. It is the most rewarding job there is. Please continue to do so for all of Us." Caesar sat back down.

Finally, it was Prophet Muhammad who stood and bowed to me. "I love you, Megan. It is perplexing to Me as to how some of Us have been written as being the furthest truth from who We are. It matters not. Every soul

A Catalyst

who enters Heaven learns the truth from involvement here with Us. Take your time as you pray to Me. Ask Me anything you like and honor Me however you like. To love Me is enough."

"I love You, Prophet Muhammad. I want You to know I will honor You in the book, and in my experiences with people who want to hear about my encounter here. You have been so kind to me and forgiving of my ignorance. I will never forget You, Prophet Muhammad. You are beautiful," I said respectfully.

God closed this occurrence with, "Archangel Michael please take Megan to the waterfall and talk about whatever she would like." At this moment Archangel Michael and I stood up from the table. He reached out His hand and I took it. We walked hand in hand across the yard to the wooden bridge where We crossed it to go and sit by the waterfall.

Chapter 19
When Time Flies

My experience in Heaven gave me many things. It gave me a clear understanding of how love truly feels. I was educated on God by, God, as to who He is. He is not an enigma to me anymore. He has a face and body that looks like He was born in Europe somewhere with an accent indicating the same. He was a gentle soul who was very kind to me despite my not having biblical knowledge, not having believed in Him or Heaven, and having strong opinions. He was love defined before me.

Heaven also introduced to me Jesus, Quan Yin, Sitting Bull, King David, Archimedes, Gaius Julius Caesar, Prophet Muhammad, Archangels, saints, and many other ascended masters who equally revere one another as they love each is to the giant equation that is Heaven.

It is my strongest of memories the stories I have shared on these pages. Each is beautiful unto itself. I do not have anyone's preference, as each is a key to the essence of love.

I have asked myself what one message it is that soars above the rest in this near-death experience; my answer is soul purpose. I believe there is more than one soul purpose each of us is born with. This soul purpose introduction for me took kidney failure to dispense such a vast amount of information I have written in this book. Blessings received Heaven for gifting me with this opportunity.

I am presently praying daily for peace to set the world free. May the harmonious convergence of duality be the defining outcome throughout humanity. Each of us is represented by love. Love is our genesis from the moment of our soul's creation. Love is the underlying formula that connects us. The science of the soul is a mathematical equation equaling 300 no matter what. Bringing me together with others in life is Holy Spirit. Holy Spirit is the reason I feel the need to link with those I encounter within my life.

Love is a fraction divided by my life's reality and multiplied by love's reality. Every day starts with me equaling a question mark. At the end of my day I know it's the energy I put into love by aligning my mind, my choice to communicate, and my soul. The energy I put into love everyday determines the answer to the question mark at the end of the day that greeted me when I woke up.

There are reasons my soul yearns to be living as my genuine self. Happiness can only be obtained when I am linked to the source of love that is my Creator.

I am a soul print in a fabric that is relativity. There is one love that is the universal soul fabric. Until this truth is accepted there will always be a snag in the universal fabric. Separating individual threads is counter intuitive.

As much as I love God, I love His Creator even more. It is the perfection of the Holy Spirit's chakra alignment or spiritual power that is the center of the universe. The

A Catalyst

center is the middle point of the sphere of all that is. The sphere is a round solid surface holding an area of activity and expertise penetrating the accompaniment of the sphere of influence that has the power to affect developments throughout every energy source existing. Each is combined and is life unified by the spinning energy that is the origin of the seven chakras. The first chakra is the root chakra representing my foundation or the character of who I am. The second chakra is the sacral chakra that is my connection to self and others. The third chakra is the solar plexus chakra that is the identity of my body. The fourth chakra is the heart chakra that is my uncontaminated connection to love. The fifth chakra is the throat chakra that is my purest form of communication to self and others. The sixth chakra is the third eye chakra and is my purest ability to connect to the source of creation, my mind. The crown chakra is my highest connection to every energy source that is greater than me or Holy Spirit.

A joining of myself can only happen by myself. It was God who told me to not look to others for their opinion of me. What matters is my opinion of myself. So, what does this mean? When I look at myself, am I only looking at the surface, or my exterior? No. I must be comfortable with how I look, but there is something much more intense. An extreme strength residing in the center of my chest. It is the location of my soul. How do I connect to my soul? I must be willing to accept every part that is, me. When I look at self, I know what is intrinsic. A higher quality of life lies within my virtues, my connection to self, my identity, knowing I am free of contamination, communication to self, connection to my mind, and my connection to the Holy Spirit. There is nothing more worthy of attention and notice.

Megan C Brown

As I am carried through each day of my life, I look to myself for the outcome of peace. I cannot look to another person to help me achieve the quality of mind I need to stay aligned with who I am. I must accomplish and bring about the resilience of my life sometimes daily. Other days are just acceptance of all that is my life. Every part of my voyage is part of the mathematical equation that surmises my being. Without the entirety of life's experience, how can I become the true elixir to my life? Life is a preparation for the afterlife. Now the question becomes, 'Why should I even care about the afterlife?' What I understand now is that my energy force is automatically linked to every other energy force. So what? What happens beyond this life of mine is much bigger. On a grand scale of all that is, I am a dot on the most beautiful golden mural that is the perfection of love I have described as Holy Spirit. This golden mural is the quintessential format of love that is woven throughout the spiritual anatomy of all that is. I would not have known this if I hadn't met with God. In a nutshell, the entire existence of every all is an aesthetically pleasing Lichtenstein painting.

The golden mural frequency compound is the alpha and omega, 000.

Scientifically the nothingness that is zero is a state alone at the heart of existentialism. Three zeros are representing the beginning, middle, and end. The beginning is the highest frequency of love, the middle is the systematic framework or main body of additional matter and illustrations that are parallel to itself. The ending consists of the absence rather than the presence of distinguishing features.

What is the highest frequency of love? It is a not previously known, revealed by God mystery of

A Catalyst

numerical sequences. A quantity of energy proportional in magnitude to the frequency of the radiation it represents. The radiation of love is equal to that of a soul. A soul unit of linear measurement of magnifying power is equal to Holy Spirit. How is this possible? Every soul is a replica of the Holy Spirit. Every soul has been born repeatedly. Each life per soul consists of different actions and reactions.

Action and reaction are individual responses. The difference is easily understood. What makes each soul the same is the numeric breakdown? It is a geometrical shape of an arch or circumference. The circumference is <.34789 over the fusion of love's center. Fusion is the process that powers the sun and the stars. It is the reaction in which two atoms of hydrogen combine, or fuse, to form an atom of helium. In the process, some of the mass of the hydrogen is converted into energy. Love's center or radius is three cubits directly below the center of the circumference. The radius being at, <.17394.5. Love's center is the point from which the activity is directed only up and side-to-side. The < symbol represents greater than. Greater than 000. In other words, a soul always can build upon the perfection of love from its inception. The beginning number of <.34789 can grow. As the arch, or circumference grows, the sides begin to grow down and toward one another eventually touching and creating a zero. When the zero is obtained and more positive energy is put into this zero, it overlaps itself and becomes stronger and stronger.

What difference does it make when zero overlaps itself and becomes stronger? It is the chain-link over itself with an unbroken line. The line can never be broken as it is the ingredients of the triple compounded love frequency. When the line grows, so too do the frequencies

Megan C Brown

of love that originate at <.34789. The entire process of growth is done in sequences of half and whole numbers only. The line never goes backward. The only way to stop the growth toward love is to communicate internally, externally, or both negativities. Negativity stops the natural flow of love.

Now that I know a little from my near-death experience about my placement of energy throughout the entire existence of the galaxies, it has become my quest as one being to imprint the Akashic records with my clean thoughts and actions in my daily life. I must regard myself as a piece of the eternal art project.

I am only one bit of energy as one soul. I am reliant on every soul's participation with me to align as a unification of love that we are created as from our inceptions. Love is our equalizer. My tie is binding with the intergalactic thread that is sewn into the spiritual anatomy. The spiritual anatomy is a structure of the internal and external workings of every living organism's energy force. My energy force is my thought patterns, my communications internally and externally, and my soul dialogue. My soul dialogue is the natural energy created as the five chambers in my ball of white energy that is my soul.

The only constant changes. Change is the foreground for self-actualizing and a constant reminder to go into a soul searching more. When I go to the aboriginal me, I am knocking on love's door. I wish I was entitled to the outcomes of my life's circumstances, but time always reveals the answers to my question of why. Faith is a necessary ingredient in personal growth.

A tool that is prayer carries me throughout the course of each day. In my mind, the word prayer once seemed to dominate a certain type of people, so I

A Catalyst

dismissed it completely. Prayer has nothing to do with religion. It is science. According to the dictionary, the truest form of prayer is an earnest request or wish. Prayer is energy, and if used in repetition, will become a powerful frequency of love. Wrong messages have rippled throughout our world. If humanity understood the power of prayer, we would breed oneness. Oneness would create tranquility and unity. Everyone must be in allegiance for prayer resulting in acceptance of difference.

Science is from Latin meaning 'knowledge.' Science is known as being a systematic enterprise for building and organizing knowledge in the form of testable explanations and predictions about the universe. Science refers to a method of knowledge itself. Science is also connected to philosophy. 'Science' and 'philosophy of nature' is sometimes used simultaneously. Natural philosophy has become, "natural science," and is considered a separate branch of philosophy. Science has been broken down in other ways as well.

Energy is a physical system of an object's state. Energy makes use of electric energy. Work performed by a given body is defined in physics as the force applied. Energy can multiply by movement and think. When energy comes up against an opposing force in a body of energy, it changes frequencies in the human body.

Frequency is a number defining the speed of movement. If a heart beats at a frequency of one hundred and twenty times a minute, its period (the interval between beats) is half a second. Traveling from one body to another, the frequency can remain the same. Frequency changes by the repetition of energy.

Repetition is doing something over, and over, and over again. In this chapter, it is the prayer I use as the example of an exercise in the mind.

Megan C Brown

Soul energy is comprised of five chambers. A complete composition of each chamber generates soul alignment. A soul is a ball of energy-containing the highest frequency of love in one location. Alignment is the moral perspective of a character, including, and making up a straight line of chakra points from top to bottom.

A chakra is an invisible point being a non-physical energy point located in every human body. There are seven chakras in total.

Science has proven exercise strengthens an area of the body being used in repetition. The energy of prayer is invisible. This repetition in the mind is a conduit to change. How can something invisible make any difference at all? My thoughts will help change the outcome of circumstances.

Laws of math and science advertise: a positive connection to a positive creates only a positive. The positive for this example is energy. Exercised positive energy results in positive change. Negatives will become invisible. When positive energy dominates, it ultimately eradicates all existing negatives.

Prayer is the act of participating in the universe for a positive outcome. Prayer is science. Not a religion. If everyone's mind thoughts, committed to creating a positive change with repetition, we are participating in prayer.

Feelings are connected to my entire being. My soul's memories constitute the exactness of each event. Everything learned before incarnating is erased at birth.

Some of the most incredible and significant souls I had only ever heard of I met in Heaven. They conveyed some of their life stories to me. I yearn for approval from every soul I was introduced to while I was there. They do

A Catalyst

not have the opportunity to come back as they were. Each is relying on me to be their voice. I pray I have spoken loud enough.

Chapter 20
Intrinsic Values

Whether or not I am aware of what is happening energetically on moment-to-moment basis matters not. What does matter is that I like who I am. I have asked myself what it means to like who I am. The word like does not fulfill what I am trying to say. What am I trying to say? I realize I must have and recognize sincere feelings. Be candid to me. Tell me the truth about how I feel about everything. Then ask me what I am feeling about everything. How is in what way do I feel. What is stating a fact about that which I am feeling. Using my near-death experience as my example I will describe it in this way. My method, or how is the orderliness of thought about the experience that I have explained throughout my book. What I have explained throughout my book communicates facts in written words. Facts according to me only as this near-death experience is the only mine to describe.

Having a distinguishing characteristic is something else I have learned to embrace. My personality is at the genesis of who I am. A harmonious feeling that is compatible between my mind and my soul, but honestly, they are not always without conflict. I have wondered if I am worthy of love, if I am right about how I accomplish my daily life, and if I am following what I know now as a result of my near-death experience.

I believe I am a participant in love on a moment-to-moment basis. When I start to lose the momentum of that which is the highest frequency of love, I stop myself in my thoughts in that moment. I like to remind myself that I am a creation of God. I have a purpose toward the enigma of my existence.

Sometimes I am at a loss for words when it comes to love. When I say I love you I am expressing at that moment to another an intense feeling of deep affection, but I have felt something more. I have felt as though I am unintentionally excluding something, but what? I decided to investigate my feeling further. I became aware of a replica of the most powerful energy being felt at that moment. It was as if a light from one celestial being came alive by the energetic transference from another. The catapulted emission of love that is a feeling beyond physical became a mystery. What will I do with this feeling?

I decided to describe this moment on paper to the soul that introduced me to this sensation. I described in words that involved two souls mirroring an energy force greater than either one had ever known was possible. I was not familiar with such a dance of energy, nor did I even know it was possible. I had to reach inside my soul dialogue for the words to come close to what I was feeling when I thought about this moment. To flourish in my soul's development as my tool navigates me toward the pivotal response of love, I believe we were brought together to ignite in one another a mysterious form of love that would not have been called to explore if it were not

A Catalyst

our time to grow spiritually. To enhance molecular compounds of enigmatic physical attraction, it must first be identified as unequivocal. What to do for me to learn God's plan of being love's mirror image, I must first investigate the reflection and recognize the self-value of my image as being only love. Then I can accept the disguise of a total circular orbit along an elliptical path around the soul. This is what I consider to be an involuntary growth toward a connection to something bigger than myself, Love.

To have given voice to a different kind of love felt unusual. Having identified it as being unlike any other feeling made me wonder about distinct love. It was recognizably different in nature than any other love I had felt before. If this can happen to me, it can happen to anyone.

How many different loves are there? There are five soul chambers I spoke of on these pages earlier. There are chambers of love as well. There is a dialogue of love, a feeling of love, communication of love, music of love, and science of love. What I shared earlier was my speaking about an emotion of love and how I had to articulate it. I did tap into the music chamber in conveying my recorded communication because it was the mind and soul connecting on paper. There were a fluent mind and soul eternal dance that transpired to write my message. The actual transmission production of raw energy materials within my soul was a quantity in the reaction of feeling I had never experienced before. It came up effortlessly resulting in an instinctive feeling I had not met yet. My automatic self-emerged uninvited from beneath the emotional rubble of my life. Now it becomes clear that what truly defines me are the chambers of love.

Megan C Brown

I had fixed action patterns in which a sequence of actions, with variation, were carried out in response to a clearly defined energy from the deepest parts of my being that were previously unforeseen because they were unknown. I did not know the whole me. I was surprised by my unexpected response. What opened was a plateau. A higher ground of being awake within my mind and soul. I was awakened by God in my near-death experience. What happened to me is best described in this way. There were ingredients, aspects of love, and influences that contributed to my outcome. Each is responsible for my change. There was no way for me to know what my outcome of change would be as a result of this encounter I share on these pages. Coming back from Heaven had immediate memories followed by years of Heaven memories uncovering the representations of the most perfect examples of love undefined on earth.

What has become different is my general attitude in life. The main elements existing in thought from my experience were uncommon but very real. Where I once enjoyed sharing my model with those closest to me, I began to refrain. I realized my feelings are out of the ordinary. I began to ask myself if it was necessary for those that I love to understand what is happening to me. My answer is no. It is a private experience God ordered me to put on these pages. He never said to share with anyone outside of this book. So, my excitement of sharing and telling my story I have brought to existence in my book.

Not only was I given my soul purpose in Heaven, but I was also linked to my intrinsic qualities that are the standard I am by love's specific format that is the formation of the golden mural representing all living energy. I realize this is heavy emotional and spiritual

A Catalyst

stuff. What is great about knowing this is heavy stuff is that I have reference now to the once enigmatic topic of God. There is no mystery for me any longer. I believe with absolute confidence.

The stuff that wonder is made of has been brought together most productively and perfectly for me. I felt as though I was being given a key to the kingdom of Heaven and I was. I was receiving all of this while lying on a hospital bed during the throws of kidney failure.

What else can I say about how this event changed my life? It brought me closer to whom I want to be and already am according to God. I am not all talked out about love though. The core of a celestial being can link to me at any given moment, but not without an invitation. Once an Archangel, Angel, saint, or ascended master has been called upon to connect to me they will. I call on every one of them every day to connect with me all at once. I have been calmed, made to feel more focused, felt a love on earth I have never experienced before, and been given a solid foundation for the daily development of my thoughts and actions.

How I move forward amid life pressures is paramount in the overall scheme of reproduction. The science of love energy admittedly sounds as if it is passive, but it is quite the contrary. I have met most of the key ingredients. God, Jesus, Prophet Muhammad, and Archangel Michael to bring some to the forefront again. It is the energy of the Holy Spirit and the actual format for love's perfect energy compound I am referring to. How I connect or disconnect to the reaction of every action. This is the key to personal development. Engaging in my life happens on a moment-to-moment basis. What I must remind myself of is the lack of engaging in anything less than love does not negate my life course. It keeps me

Megan C Brown

neutral. I do not help or support negativity or positivity. Supporting positivity for me is daily conscious work. I make it a point to invest my energy by thought and action toward love with my responsibilities, prayer, random acts of kindness, and calling my friends.

I grew up hearing the name God. This name is universal, but what does it mean? Every name has a meaning. It was defined in Heaven for me this way. G stands for 'geodetics' that is a branch of applied mathematics and sciences. It is the scientific regulation that deals with the measurement and representation of every all. O stands for 'obsolete' indicating it is a part of an organism in a related species. D stands for 'dogma' that is a set of principles laid down by an authority. God is the exact image of the Absolute Creator, Love. The Absolute Creator is Holy Spirit and is the Love energy making up the human-looking form that is God. God is the absolute likeness of being each of us is.

I am saying each of us is GOD, but only spelled in all capital letters. We are each a branch of applied mathematics and sciences, we are each in a related species, and we are a set of principles laid down by God, the authority.

The image of God is who we are as humans. As an image, we are a representation of the internal and external form of God or the likeness of God. How beautiful it is to know the purest form of love created a being that is God whom we as humanity represent.

To make the statement humanity is GOD is not a violation or misuse of what is sacred, God. I intend to position upon these pages the beauty of the connection between all of us and our Creator.

It has become clear to me to God, all things are possible. It has become clear to me with GOD, all things

A Catalyst

are also possible. I have come to understand the saying in the Bible, "image of God." We are a replica of God. We are scientifically and genetically structured with the same ingredients. The obvious difference is God is our ruler; as a ruler who is linked to Holy Spirit whose love frequency is at an all-time high, God is relieved of the pettiness of quarrels. God is determined to link all of humanity to the underlying capabilities that are the natural origin of our soul. Every soul was created by Holy Spirit to be a replica of love repeatedly. Our soul creation had only one wish attached to its creation, love. What God gave every soul in human form was the gift of choice. With every incarnation of every soul's fingerprint or soul groove of every choice was the determining factor that is the difference. This difference I am writing about has determined the separation of humanity amongst itself and God.

If humanity was to use the original format of creation as its baseline, we could reverse the imprint of every soul groove. What this means is the eradication of difference despite choice. What will ultimately accompany every soul choice is acceptance of one another despite our differences. As God, Jesus, Archangel Michael, and Prophet Muhammad once said to me, "Acceptance is synonymous with love."

I am an ever-changing enigma to myself on an everyday basis due to life. I do not know what will happen on a moment-to-moment basis, but I do know whatever happens will require of me absolute faith in love. I must, no matter the circumstances, be willing to allow my mindset to be in love. I must not allow every emotionless than love to dictate the course of my day which could domino into my future in ways I have no way of knowing. So, I must keep it simple. I must choose to use a personal dialogue that is cognizant of every life alive around me. Something like, "Love divides no one. I only want a higher platform for loves different displays of being my guide at this moment to be felt by my entire being. May I shine forth that which is the origin of who I am, love? Be with me in this now God and Heaven, and direct my focus to the almighty Creator, Holy Spirit. May loves the greatest originator be the recipient of my troubles and worries and diffuse them so as not to interrupt the rhythm of loves cadence throughout every all."

Life is linear despite what anyone says. We are linear beings from the moment of our souls' creation. Creation is a progression from one stage to another in a single series of steps, and it is sequential. There is absolute order in all creation. Without order there is chaos. Each of us is a mirror reflection of science that is our Creator. Our Creator is love. Love is divided by ingredients of scientific specificities only. We are orderly patterns of metabolic and developmental reactions. We are characteristic properties of living organisms. We are individuals bound to one another by loves energy. Just as a ring fits perfectly on a finger, our molecules given at our creation have mirror-image forms allowing each to bind to one another a specific quality and state of being. From the moment of our creation is thought. This has never been included as a part of our conception. It is always about the heartbeat.

The thought is beyond the brain; the brain is an organ contained in the skull and acts as the coordinating center of sensation and intellectual and nervous activity. There is another brain called the soul's brain. An enigmatic house of information connected to the Akashic Records. These Akashic Records are the be-all and end all of life's central position of information. Not just one life,

A Catalyst

every life every soul has lived. The soul is a communication link to Holy Spirit. Why does Holy Spirit need a brain to communicate with when all love frequencies vibrate at a higher purpose than anything humanity has ever created? The vibration is that of falsetto sung by Archangels in Heaven. What this means is humanity is also intertwined with Celestial Beings that have been attached to earth since the beginning of mankind. Each Celestial Being is a part of the golden thread creating the fabric of every throughout the universe. The threads of every life lived have created a seamless tapestry of love that blankets each of us. The soul's brain vibrates to a registered chord of love that is 'b' triple sharp, and 'c' triple sharp. Those who play the notes daily will open a direct link to love's messages. The soul has then ignited automatically as a result of playing three octaves of these two notes simultaneously. The more often these notes are played, the stronger a soul's connection will be to its Creator, Love.

Archangels are simply specialists in Their field. Archangel Michael defeats evil and serves as a warrior and advocate for Israel. Archangel Raphael performs all manners of healing. Archangel Gabriel announced the forthcoming births of John the Baptist and Jesus Christ and is the supreme Messenger of God. There is an Archangel for every way of being. The common Ones are Archangel Metatron known as the Recording Angel. Archangel Raziel is known as Keeper of the Secrets, or privacy of the mind. Archangel Jophiel is the Archangel of Beauty. It is Her mission to bring beauty to all aspects of life including, thoughts, feelings, home and office, and personal self. Archangel Tzaphkiel works to help people know more about God so they can better understand Him. Archangel Tzadkiel is the Archangel of freedom, benevolence, mercy, and the Patron Angel of all who forgives. Archangel Khamael gives energy and courage and is the heart chakra. Archangel Haniel represents our inner world of intuition, imagination, and emotions. Archangel Uriel protects humankind from evil. Archangel Sandalphon is the ruling Angel and protector of earth.

Humanity is inner connected to love in ways it has not known to give credence to. While I am getting ready to sleep at night, I always call upon the Celestial souls that come to my mind. I ask them to be with me as I sleep and bring forth in my life that which is for the highest good. Love, faith, and mercy. The almighty energy, complete trust and confidence in Holy Spirit, God, and Heaven, compassion, and forgiveness to everyone. With these key ingredients, I am an active participant in the Holy Trinity. It is compassion, a concern for others that will automatically activate acceptance.

A life lived in fear is no life at all. A life lived in compassion will never exclude. As acceptance is synonymous with love, so too is love to everyone. In the end is when we find out with great certainty love was never a gender, color of skin, or religion. It was and is the most amazing way of being given to us at our life's conception. As Dr. Martin Luther King, Jr. said, 'In a sense, we have come to our nation's capital to cash a check. When the architects of our republic wrote the magnificent words of the Constitution and the Declaration of Independence, they were signing a promissory note to which every American was to fall heir. This note was a promise that all men would be guaranteed the inalienable rights of life, liberty, and the pursuit of happiness.'

A Catalyst

Respectfully I will use my inspiration from Dr. King's speech and say, "I have a dream for our world to come to a philosophical realization. When the architect that is love created the magnificent reality that all men and women are created equal, it was to fall heir to everyone. Every individual creation is guaranteed the inalienable rights of life, liberty, and the pursuit of happiness. May the forthcoming fundamental knowledge, reality, and existence be to serve love. This is always Heaven's dream."

Poem:
The Power of One

It is solemn and majestic. It holds a space so vast the human mind cannot fathom measurement. It's powerful force cannot be tamed. It's strong emotion can cause physical power to move quickly in a calm manner. Its path is pure. It's source for ignition is you. A soul reflecting back a clear image twinning love. The magnificence of your display has created within me an imported energy completely covering my soul. I am consumed with love. You have lit the fire for the one wick in the core of my being.

I vow to honor the harmony you have introduced me to. A climax within I will never relinquish. You radiate that which I feel in undiscovered depths of emotions. You

Megan C Brown

have bestowed me with a vulnerability I will embrace
eternally. I am unable to touch you, but my memory
mirrors for me a condition of pleasure immeasurable to
any other feeling I know. Your touch upon me has
transformed my ability to respond with a quality of
being open I didn't know before you.

My inability to walk away from you is permanent. I feel
as if I have been awarded with the greatest treasure I
could ever receive. Your impact, love, has paralyzed my
mind to ever want for anything more.

Acknowledgements

I want to fully express my gratitude to some beautiful people who have touched my soul. I have met each of you in my life before and since my near-death experience. I have felt love from each of you.

Gina, Larry, Karen, Yerevan, Shekina, Stacy, Stephanie, and Leslie. Each of you has shared pieces of your life with me. You have always been a part of what I consider to be my soul family, and I will always love you. Blessings received to each of you for sharing with me your kindness, generosity, compassion, and love.

Made in the USA
Middletown, DE
20 June 2024